OPPOSING
VIEWPOINTS®
SERIES

# Corporate
# Social Responsibility

*Susan Hunnicutt, Book Editor*

**GREENHAVEN PRESS**
*A part of Gale, Cengage Learning*

GALE
CENGAGE Learning˙

Detroit • New York • San Francisco • New Haven, Conn • Waterville, Maine • London

Christine Nasso, *Publisher*
Elizabeth Des Chenes, *Managing Editor*

© 2009 Greenhaven Press, a part of Gale, Cengage Learning.

Gale and Greenhaven Press are registered trademarks used herein under license.

*For more information, contact:*
Greenhaven Press
27500 Drake Rd.
Farmington Hills, MI 48331-3535
Or you can visit our Internet site at gale.cengage.com

For product information and technology assistance, contact us at

Gale Customer Support, 1-800-877-4253
For permission to use material from this text or product, submit all requests online at www.cengage.com/permissions

Further permissions questions can be emailed to permissionrequest@cengage.com

Articles in Greenhaven Press anthologies are often edited for length to meet page requirements. In addition, original titles of these works are changed to clearly present the main thesis and to explicitly indicate the author's opinion. Every effort is made to ensure that Greenhaven Press accurately reflects the original intent of the authors. Every effort has been made to trace the owners of copyrighted material.

Cover photograph reproduced by © Ettore Marzochhi, 2009/Istockphoto.com.

LIBRARY OF CONGRESS CATALOGING-IN-PUBLICATION DATA

Corporate social responsibility / Susan Hunnicutt, book editor.
    p. cm. -- (Opposing viewpoints)
    Includes bibliographical references and index.
    ISBN 978-0-7377-4230-5 (hardcover)
    ISBN 978-0-7377-4231-2 (pbk.)
    1. Social responsibility of business. 2. Corporate culture. I. Hunnicutt, Susan.
    HD60.C6913 2009
    658.4'08--dc22
                                                        2008050586

Printed in the United States of America
1 2 3 4 5 6 7 13 12 11 10 09

# Contents

## Chapter 3: Do Corporations Have a Social Responsibility to Protect Human Rights?

## Chapter 4: What Factors Are Influencing Corporations to Behave More Responsibly?

# Why Consider Opposing Viewpoints?

> *"The only way in which a human being can make some approach to knowing the whole of a subject is by hearing what can be said about it by persons of every variety of opinion and studying all modes in which it can be looked at by every character of mind. No wise man ever acquired his wisdom in any mode but this."*
>
> *John Stuart Mill*

In our media-intensive culture it is not difficult to find differing opinions. Thousands of newspapers and magazines and dozens of radio and television talk shows resound with differing points of view. The difficulty lies in deciding which opinion to agree with and which "experts" seem the most credible. The more inundated we become with differing opinions and claims, the more essential it is to hone critical reading and thinking skills to evaluate these ideas. Opposing Viewpoints books address this problem directly by presenting stimulating debates that can be used to enhance and teach these skills. The varied opinions contained in each book examine many different aspects of a single issue. While examining these conveniently edited opposing views, readers can develop critical thinking skills such as the ability to compare and contrast authors' credibility, facts, argumentation styles, use of persuasive techniques, and other stylistic tools. In short, the Opposing Viewpoints Series is an ideal way to attain the higher-level thinking and reading skills so essential in a culture of diverse and contradictory opinions.

In addition to providing a tool for critical thinking, Opposing Viewpoints books challenge readers to question their own strongly held opinions and assumptions. Most people form their opinions on the basis of upbringing, peer pressure, and personal, cultural, or professional bias. By reading carefully balanced opposing views, readers must directly confront new ideas as well as the opinions of those with whom they disagree. This is not to simplistically argue that everyone who reads opposing views will—or should—change his or her opinion. Instead, the series enhances readers' understanding of their own views by encouraging confrontation with opposing ideas. Careful examination of others' views can lead to the readers' understanding of the logical inconsistencies in their own opinions, perspective on why they hold an opinion, and the consideration of the possibility that their opinion requires further evaluation.

## Evaluating Other Opinions

To ensure that this type of examination occurs, Opposing Viewpoints books present all types of opinions. Prominent spokespeople on different sides of each issue as well as well-known professionals from many disciplines challenge the reader. An additional goal of the series is to provide a forum for other, less known, or even unpopular viewpoints. The opinion of an ordinary person who has had to make the decision to cut off life support from a terminally ill relative, for example, may be just as valuable and provide just as much insight as a medical ethicist's professional opinion. The editors have two additional purposes in including these less known views. One, the editors encourage readers to respect others' opinions—even when not enhanced by professional credibility. It is only by reading or listening to and objectively evaluating others' ideas that one can determine whether they are worthy of consideration. Two, the inclusion of such viewpoints encourages the important critical thinking skill of ob-

jectively evaluating an author's credentials and bias. This evaluation will illuminate an author's reasons for taking a particular stance on an issue and will aid in readers' evaluation of the author's ideas.

It is our hope that these books will give readers a deeper understanding of the issues debated and an appreciation of the complexity of even seemingly simple issues when good and honest people disagree. This awareness is particularly important in a democratic society such as ours in which people enter into public debate to determine the common good. Those with whom one disagrees should not be regarded as enemies but rather as people whose views deserve careful examination and may shed light on one's own.

Thomas Jefferson once said that "difference of opinion leads to inquiry, and inquiry to truth." Jefferson, a broadly educated man, argued that "if a nation expects to be ignorant and free ... it expects what never was and never will be." As individuals and as a nation, it is imperative that we consider the opinions of others and examine them with skill and discernment. The Opposing Viewpoints Series is intended to help readers achieve this goal.

*David L. Bender and Bruno Leone,*
*Founders*

# Introduction

> *"The extraordinary wealth creation of recent years has produced a large number of extremely rich people, many of them from the software and finance industries, who are interested in a new kind of philanthropy . . . It involves using money for maximum impact by investing in potentially disruptive technologies . . . and in social enterprises that can be scaled up as required."*
>
> The Economist,
> *January, 2008*

In early 2008 Bill Gates, founder and chairman of the Microsoft Corporation, addressed the annual World Economic Forum in Davos, Switzerland. Delivering what he called "the most important speech I will make this year," Gates spoke of a "hybrid engine of self-interest and concern for others [that] can serve a much wider circle than can be reached by self-interest or caring alone." He urged his listeners to adopt new ways of thinking about the success of their business endeavors: As entrepreneurial leaders, they should be concerned not only about generating profits, but also about finding ways to improve the lives of impoverished people around the world.

Later, Gates continued the conversation in an essay in *Time* magazine. "It is mainly corporations that have the skills to make technological innovations work for the poor," he wrote. "To make the most of those skills, we need a more creative capitalism; an attempt to stretch the reach of market forces so that more companies can benefit from doing work that makes more people better off. We need new ways to bring far more people into the system—capitalism—that has done so much good in the world."

Creative capitalism as it has been articulated by Bill Gates is the most recent instance of the corporate social responsibility (CSR) movement that has become increasingly prominent in the international business community in recent years. Examples of creative capitalism highlighted by Gates include Microsoft's commitment to bring wireless communication to impoverished third world communities, and also its efforts to develop a personal computing interface that would allow illiterate or semi-literate people to use a computer with very little training.

Gates also cited recent initiatives by the World Health Organization (WHO) to procure vaccinations for meningitis and cholera that would be affordable in third world settings. In each of these instances, WHO, after determining what prices would be affordable for targeted communities, was able to persuade drug manufacturers to produce the vaccines, and to make them available at very low cost. These projects and others like them are undertaken not primarily in order to produce profits, but because of a belief that they will make the world a better place.

As Gates explained in the *Time* article, "Businesses . . . can benefit from the public recognition and enhanced reputation that come from serving those who can't pay." Socially responsible behavior is seen as value that is added to a product, and can be "the tipping point that leads people to pick one product over another."

The idea that human beings are motivated by genuine concern for the interests of others is a key concept of the corporate social responsibility movement. In his speech before the World Economic Forum in Davos, Gates quoted Adam Smith, author of *The Wealth of Nations* and the father of capitalist thought: *"How selfish soever man may be supposed, there are evidently some principles in his nature, which interest him in the fortunes of others, and render their happiness necessary to him, though he derives nothing from it, except the pleasure of*

*seeing it.*" When Gates elaborated on the concept of creative capitalism by quoting Adam Smith, it was a way of arguing that CSR initiatives can coincide with basic capitalist principles.

Gates's vision is controversial, however. While his speech in Davos took place before a standing room only audience of international executives, a senior editor for *Fortune* magazine reported later that his remarks were greeted with "tepid applause," and a "merely polite reception." Creative capitalism also draws criticism from outside the business community, from individuals who believe that the social responsibilities of corporations are too important to be left to the benevolent impulses of CEOs and boards of directors.

Champions of what might be called a more traditional capitalist perspective believe that "the business of business is business." For them, instigators of CSR initiatives like those described by Gates are guilty of theft, since they must fund their idealistic ventures with money that belongs to investors. This was the position taken by two economists, Philip Coelho and James McClure, in a response to Gates's Davos speech that appeared in the Fort Wayne, Indiana, *News-Sentinel.* "Firms were incorporated for the express pursuit of enhancing their owners' economic well-being. . . ." Coelho and McClure wrote. "The doctrine of corporate social responsibility fosters extra-legal expropriations of stockholders' wealth; if stockholders wanted to simply give their money away, they would not have bought stock." Coehlo and McClure are troubled by the extent to which the rhetoric of CSR has permeated the academic community, and the extent to which that community has lent its authority to a position they view as a distortion of basic principles of business ethics.

Gates's vision of creative capitalism and corporate social responsibility has also been criticized by those who say that justice is too important to be left to the whims of the business community. "Gates writes that if companies are going to get

more involved [in CSR initiatives and creative capitalism], they need some kind of return . . ." says Stephen Dick, in an August 2008 response to the *Time* magazine article. "[Gates says] 'It's about giving (corporations) a real incentive to apply their expertise in new ways making it possible to earn a return while serving the people who have been left out.'" But for Dick, "Those who were left out were forcibly left out by a predatory . . . system that treats workers as expendable, spends millions to prevent union start-ups, leaves behind empty factories and the pollution below so taxpayers can clean up the mess, and the sorry list goes on. . . ." Dick feels that CSR initiatives like creative capitalism are nothing more than window dressing; that they divert attention from an unjust system, and leave outside the law matters of fundamental fairness that need to be determined under the law. According to Dick, government has an important role to play, by actively pushing for "unions and increased taxation on businesses . . . and policies . . . that will temper the excesses of capitalism and rein in the power of corporations. . . ."

The questions that emerge at the intersections of these three positions—of Gates, of Coehlo and McClure, and of Dick—are representative of the ongoing discussion about the social responsibility of business: Is it a good thing for corporations to voluntarily undertake humanitarian projects, or projects to protect the environment from harm, and to use company revenues to finance them? Or are such projects a misuse of profits that actually belong to investors? Conversely, do CSR initiatives satisfy a corporation's debt to society, or do they deflect attention from matters of justice that should be settled under the law, and not left to the benevolence of CEOs and boards of directors? Questions like these are addressed from a variety of points of view in *Opposing Viewpoints: Corporate Social Responsibility* in the following chapters: What Is Corporate Social Responsibility? How Have Corporations Been Impacted by Concerns About the Environment? Do Corpora-

tions Have a Responsibility to Respect Human Rights? and What Factors Are Influencing Corporations to Behave More Responsibly? Each of these chapters define the boundaries of a broad range of issues that together are encompassed by the notion of corporate social responsibility.

CHAPTER 1

# What Is Corporate
# Social Responsibility?

# Chapter Preface

The classic economic description of the corporation assumes two things: first, shareholders—owners of company stock—are interested only in maximizing the financial value of their investments; and second, when evaluating the success of a company the investors' desires for financial gain are the only desires that really matter. A corporation is responsible when it is a good steward of funds entrusted to it by investors.

In recent discussions of corporate social responsibility, controversy often develops because parties to the conversation differ over whether these two assumptions are correct. In addition to investors, advocates of corporate social responsibility typically recognize other important stakeholders, including employees and members of communities, who have a legitimate interest in the direction of the company. In addition to financial profits, advocates of corporate social responsibility also recognize other kinds of value that can be produced by corporate enterprises, such as strengthened workforces, healthier communities, and a more secure natural environment.

A recent *Wall Street Journal* article told the story of Stephanie Runyan, a 36-year-old industrial psychologist who completed a six-month working sabbatical in Nairobi, Kenya, that was paid for by her employer, the consulting firm Accenture. Runyan's story provides a useful illustration. While in Kenya, Runyan developed a training program for nurses. The training was provided by Accenture to the Kenyan nurses at a greatly reduced rate, through its Employee Development Program. While the arrangement almost certainly represented a financial loss, it was profitable in other ways. According to the article, before her sabbatical Runyan had been considering leaving her job; in Kenya, she had a satisfying work experience

and a needed break from her regular employment. Through the sabbatical experience, Accenture was able to recognize, reward, and possibly retain a valued employee. Finally, the Kenyan nurses who received the training were able to benefit from Accenture's consulting services and Runyan's professional expertise at a cost that was affordable for them.

The desire of employees for meaningful work experiences—experiences that offer "more than a paycheck"—is one force that is pushing firms to think in a broader way about the definition of commercial success and the meaning of corporate social responsibility. A 2006 study showed that environmental awareness and a proactive response to issues like poverty and disease in the developing world are key factors in the way a company is evaluated by prospective employees. Seventy-nine percent of those surveyed said they want to work for a company that cares about how it impacts and contributes to society; 64 percent say that a company's social/environmental activities make them feel more loyal.

Do companies exist solely in order to maximize the "bottom line" or are there other values that should be considered in reflecting on the success or failure of a commercial enterprise? Is it right for a company to consider the desires of workers and community members or are the desires of investors the only desires that really matter? Is the positive impact of programs like Accenture's Employee Development Program on its workforce enough to merit the cost of the program?

Exactly what does it mean for corporations to be socially responsible? Often, individual opinions of corporate social responsibility, and whether it is a good or bad thing for the business community, come down to questions about what is judged to be valuable, and for whom. These are the questions that will be considered in this chapter.

"[We] *offer this exchange as the starting point of a discussion that should be intensely important to all devotees of free minds and free markets.*"

# The Purpose of Social Responsibility Is Open to Debate

*John Mackey*

*In this collection of viewpoints John Mackey, founder of Whole Foods Market, debates the definition of social responsibility and the proper role of corporations with Nobel Prize-winning economist Milton Friedman and Cypress Semiconductor's founder and CEO, T.J. Rodgers. Mackey and Rodgers are both successful businessmen. Friedman, who died in 2006, a short time after this conversation took place, was the author of an article that became a classic text in the field of corporate social responsibility. That article, "The Social Responsibility of Business Is to Increase Its Profits," first appeared in* The New York Times Magazine *in 1970.*

John Mackey, "Rethinking the Social Responsibility of Business," in *Reason* magazine and Reason.com, October 2005. Reproduced by permission.

As you read, consider the following questions:

1. According to John Mackey, Whole Foods has six groups of stakeholders, one of which is investors. Who are the other five stakeholders Mackey lists?

2. Why does Milton Friedman think that corporate philanthropy is not a clearly defined good?

3. What does T.J. Rogers mean by the "demonstrated social benefit of 'self-interest'"? What are some goods that might be the result of "self interest"?

Thirty-five years ago, Milton Friedman wrote a famous article for *The New York Times Magazine* whose title aptly summed up its main point: "The Social Responsibility of Business Is to Increase Its Profits." The future Nobel laureate in economics had no patience for capitalists who claimed that "business is not concerned 'merely' with profit but also with promoting desirable 'social' ends; that business has a 'social conscience' and takes seriously its responsibilities for providing employment, eliminating discrimination, avoiding pollution and whatever else may be the catchwords of the contemporary crop of reformers."

Friedman . . . wrote that such people are "preaching pure and unadulterated socialism. Businessmen who talk this way are unwitting puppets of the intellectual forces that have been undermining the basis of a free society these past decades."

John Mackey, the founder and CEO of Whole Foods, is one businessman who disagrees with Friedman. A self-described ardent libertarian whose conversation is peppered with references to [economist] Ludwig von Mises and [psychologist] Abraham Maslow, Austrian economics and astrology, Mackey believes Friedman's view is too narrow a description of his and many other businesses' activities. As important, he argues that Friedman's take woefully undersells the humanitarian dimension of capitalism.

In the debate that follows, Mackey lays out his personal vision of the social responsibility of business. Friedman responds, as does T.J. Rodgers, the founder and CEO of Cypress Semiconductor and the chief spokesman of what might be called the tough love school of laissez faire [a policy of allowing events to take their own course without interference]. Dubbed "one of America's toughest bosses" by *Fortune*, Rodgers argues that corporations add far more to society by maximizing "long-term shareholder value" than they do by donating time and money to charity.

*Reason* offers this exchange as the starting point of a discussion that should be intensely important to all devotees of free minds and free markets.

## Putting Customers Ahead of Investors: John Mackey

In 1970 Milton Friedman wrote that "there is one and only one social responsibility of business—to use its resources and engage in activities designed to increase its profits so long as it stays within the rules of the game, which is to say, engages in open and free competition without deception or fraud." That's the orthodox view among free market economists: that the only social responsibility a law-abiding business has is to maximize profits for the shareholders.

I strongly disagree. I'm a businessman and a free market libertarian, but I believe that the enlightened corporation should try to create value for *all* of its constituencies. From an investor's perspective, the purpose of the business is to maximize profits. But that's not the purpose for other stakeholders—for customers, employees, suppliers, and the community. Each of those groups will define the purpose of the business in terms of its own needs and desires, and each perspective is valid and legitimate.

My argument should not be mistaken for a hostility to profit. I believe I know something about creating shareholder

value. When I co-founded Whole Foods Market 27 years ago, we began with $45,000 in capital; we only had $250,000 in sales our first year. During the last 12 months we had sales of more than $4.6 billion, net profits of more than $160 million, and a market capitalization over $8 billion.

But we have not achieved our tremendous increase in shareholder value by making shareholder value the primary purpose of our business. In my marriage, my wife's happiness is an end in itself, not merely a means to my own happiness; love leads me to put my wife's happiness first, but in doing so I also make myself happier. Similarly, the most successful businesses put the customer first, ahead of the investors. In the profit-centered business, customer happiness is merely a means to an end: maximizing profits. In the customer-centered business, customer happiness is an end in itself, and will be pursued with greater interest, passion, and empathy than the profit-centered business is capable of.

## We Create Value for All Our Stakeholders

Not that we're only concerned with customers. At Whole Foods, we measure our success by how much value we can create for all six of our most important stakeholders: customers, team members (employees), investors, vendors, communities, and the environment.

There is, of course, no magical formula to calculate how much value each stakeholder should receive from the company. It is a dynamic process that evolves with the competitive marketplace. No stakeholder remains satisfied for long. It is the function of company leadership to develop solutions that continually work for the common good.

Many thinking people will readily accept my arguments that caring about customers and employees is good business. But they might draw the line at believing a company has any responsibility to its community and environment. To donate time and capital to philanthropy, they will argue, is to steal

from the investors. After all, the corporation's assets legally belong to the investors, don't they? Management has a fiduciary responsibility to maximize shareholder value; therefore, any activities that don't maximize shareholder value are violations of this duty. If you feel altruism towards other people, you should exercise that altruism with your own money, not with the assets of a corporation that doesn't belong to you.

This position sounds reasonable. A company's assets do belong to the investors, and its management does have a duty to manage those assets responsibly. In my view, the argument is not *wrong* so much as it is too narrow.

First, there can be little doubt that a certain amount of corporate philanthropy is simply good business and works for the long-term benefit of the investors. For example: In addition to the many thousands of small donations each Whole Foods store makes each year, we also hold five 5% Days throughout the year. On those days, we donate 5 percent of a store's total sales to a nonprofit organization. While our stores select worthwhile organizations to support, they also tend to focus on groups that have large membership lists, which are contacted and encouraged to shop our store that day to support the organization. This usually brings hundreds of new or lapsed customers into our stores, many of whom then become regular shoppers. So a 5% Day not only allows us to support worthwhile causes, but is an excellent marketing strategy that has benefited Whole Foods investors immensely.

## Entrepreneurs Define the Company

That said, I believe such programs would be completely justifiable even if they produced no profits and no P.R. [publicity]. This is because I believe the entrepreneurs, not the current investors in a company's stock, have the right and responsibility to define the purpose of the company. It is the entrepreneurs who create a company, who bring all the factors of production together and coordinate it into viable business. It is the entre-

preneurs who set the company strategy and who negotiate the terms of trade with all of the voluntarily cooperating stake-holders—including the investors. At Whole Foods we "hired" our original investors. They didn't hire us.

We first announced that we would donate 5 percent of the company's net profits to philanthropy when we drafted our mission statement, back in 1985. Our policy has therefore been in place for over 20 years, and it predates our IPO [initial public offering] by seven years. All seven of the private investors at the time we created the policy voted for it when they served on our board of directors. When we took in venture capital money back in 1989, none of the venture firms objected to the policy. In addition, in almost 14 years as a publicly traded company, almost no investors have ever raised objections to the policy. How can Whole Foods' philanthropy be "theft" from the current investors if the original owners of the company unanimously approved the policy and all subsequent investors made their investments after the policy was in effect and well publicized? . . .

When we are small children we are egocentric, concerned only about our own needs and desires. As we mature, most people grow beyond this egocentrism and begin to care about others—their families, friends, communities, and countries. Our capacity to love can expand even further: to loving people from different races, religions, and countries—potentially to unlimited love for all people and even for other sentient creatures. This is our potential as human beings, to take joy in the flourishing of people everywhere. Whole Foods gives money to our communities because we care about them and feel a responsibility to help them flourish as well as possible.

The business model that Whole Foods has embraced could represent a new form of capitalism, one that more consciously works for the common good instead of depending solely on the "invisible hand" to generate positive results for society. The "brand" of capitalism is in terrible shape throughout the

"Make sure everything is done ethically. Within reason, of course." Cartoon by Andrew Toos. www.CartoonStock.com.

world, and corporations are widely seen as selfish, greedy, and uncaring. This is both unfortunate and unnecessary, and could be changed if businesses and economists widely adopted the business model that I have outlined here.

To extend our love and care beyond our narrow self-interest is antithetical to neither our human nature nor our financial success. Rather, it leads to the further fulfillment of both. Why do we not encourage this in our theories of business and economics? Why do we restrict our theories to such a pessimistic and crabby view of human nature? What are we afraid of?

## Making Philanthropy Out of Obscenity: Milton Friedman

> *By pursuing his own interest [an individual] frequently promotes that of the society more effectually than when he really*

*intends to promote it. I have never known much good done by*
*those who affected to trade for the public good.*

—Adam Smith, *The Wealth of Nations*

The differences between John Mackey and me regarding the social responsibility of business are for the most part rhetorical. Strip off the camouflage, and it turns out we are in essential agreement. Moreover, his company, Whole Foods Market, behaves in accordance with the principles I spelled out in my 1970 *New York Times Magazine* article.

With respect to his company, it could hardly be otherwise. It has done well in a highly competitive industry. Had it devoted any significant fraction of its resources to exercising a social responsibility unrelated to the bottom line, it would be out of business by now or would have been taken over.

Here is how Mackey himself describes his firm's activities:

1. "The most successful businesses put the customer first, instead of the investors" (which clearly means that this is the way to put the investors first).

2. "There can be little doubt that a certain amount of corporate philanthropy is simply good business and works for the long-term benefit of the investors."

Compare this to what I wrote in 1970:

"Of course, in practice the doctrine of social responsibility is frequently a cloak for actions that are justified on other grounds rather than a reason for those actions.

"To illustrate, it may well be in the long run interest of a corporation that is a major employer in a small community to devote resources to providing amenities to that community or to improving its government. . . .

"In each of these . . . cases, there is a strong temptation to rationalize these actions as an exercise of 'social responsibility.' In the present climate of opinion, with its widespread aversion to 'capitalism,' 'profits,' the 'soulless corporation' and so on,

this is one way for a corporation to generate goodwill as a by-product of expenditures that are entirely justified in its own self-interest.

"It would be inconsistent of me to call on corporate executives to refrain from this hypocritical window-dressing because it harms the foundations of a free society. That would be to call on them to exercise a 'social responsibility'! If our institutions and the attitudes of the public make it in their self-interest to cloak their actions in this way, I cannot summon much indignation to denounce them."

## We Disagree About What Is Good

I believe Mackey's flat statement that "corporate philanthropy is a good thing" is flatly wrong. Consider the decision by the founders of Whole Foods to donate 5 percent of net profits to philanthropy. They were clearly within their rights in doing so. They were spending their own money, using 5 percent of one part of their wealth to establish, thanks to corporate tax provisions, the equivalent of a 501c(3) charitable foundation, though with no mission statement, no separate by-laws, and no provision for deciding on the beneficiaries. But what reason is there to suppose that the stream of profit distributed in this way would do more good for society than investing that stream of profit in the enterprise itself or paying it out as dividends and letting the stockholders dispose of it? The practice makes sense only because of our obscene tax laws, whereby a stockholder can make a larger gift for a given after-tax cost if the corporation makes the gift on his behalf than if he makes the gift directly. That is a good reason for eliminating the corporate tax or for eliminating the deductibility of corporate charity, but it is not a justification for corporate charity.

Whole Foods Market's contribution to society—and as a customer I can testify that it is an important one—is to enhance the pleasure of shopping for food. Whole Foods has no

special competence in deciding how charity should be distributed. Any funds devoted to the latter would surely have contributed more to society if they had been devoted to improving still further the former.

Finally, I shall try to explain why my statement that "the social responsibility of business [is] to increase its profits" and Mackey's statement that "the enlightened corporation should try to create value for all of its constituencies" are equivalent.

Note first that I refer to *social* responsibility, not financial, or accounting, or legal. It is social precisely to allow for the constituencies to which Mackey refers. Maximizing profits is an end from the private point of view; it is a means from the social point of view. A system based on private property and free markets is a sophisticated means of enabling people to cooperate in their economic activities without compulsion; it enables separated knowledge to assure that each resource is used for its most valued use, and is combined with other resources in the most efficient way.

Of course, this is abstract and idealized. The world is not ideal. There are all sorts of deviations from the perfect market—many, if not most, I suspect, due to government interventions. But with all its defects, the current largely free-market, private-property world seems to me vastly preferable to a world in which a large fraction of resources is used and distributed by 501c(3)s and their corporate counterparts.

## Put Profits First: T.J. Rodgers

John Mackey's article attacking corporate profit maximization could not have been written by "a free market libertarian," as claimed. Indeed, if the examples he cites had not identified him as the author, one could easily assume the piece was written by [political activist] Ralph Nader. A more accurate title for his article is "How Business and Profit Making Fit Into My Overarching Philosophy of Altruism."

Mackey spouts nonsense about how his company hired his original investors, not vice versa. If Whole Foods ever falls on persistent hard times—perhaps when the Luddites are no longer able to hold back the genetic food revolution using junk science and fear—he will quickly find out who has hired whom, as his investors fire him.

Mackey does make one point that is consistent with, but not supportive of, free market capitalism. He knows that shareholders own his stock voluntarily. If they don't like the policies of his company, they can always vote to change those policies with a shareholder resolution or simply sell the stock and buy that of another company more aligned with their objectives. Thus, he informs his shareholders of his objectives and lets them make a choice on which stock to buy. So far, so good.

It is also simply good business for a company to cater to its customers, train and retain its employees, build long-term positive relationships with its suppliers, and become a good citizen in its community, including performing some philanthropic activity. When Milton Friedman says a company should stay "within the rules of the game" and operate "without deception or fraud," he means it should deal with all its various constituencies properly in order to maximize long-term shareholder value. He does not mean that a company should put every last nickel on the bottom line every quarter, regardless of the long-term consequences.

My company, Cypress Semiconductor, has won the trophy for the Second Harvest Food Bank competition for the most food donated per employee in Silicon Valley for the last 13 consecutive years (1 million pounds of food in 2004). The contest creates competition among our divisions, leading to employee involvement, company food drives, internal social events with admissions "paid for" by food donations, and so forth. It is a big employee morale builder, a way to attract new employees, good P.R. for the company, and a significant ben-

efit to the community—all of which makes Cypress a better place to work and invest in. Indeed, Mackey's own proud example of Whole Foods' community involvement programs also made a profit.

## Self-Interest Is a Social Good

But Mackey's subordination of his profession as a businessman to altruistic ideals shows up as he attempts to negate the empirically demonstrated social benefit of "self-interest" by defining it narrowly as "increasing short-term profits." Why is it that when Whole Foods gives money to a worthy cause, it serves a high moral objective, while a company that provides a good return to small investors—who simply put their money into their own retirement funds or a children's college fund—is somehow selfish? It's the philosophy that is objectionable here, not the specific actions. If Mackey wants to run a hybrid business/charity whose mission is fully disclosed to his shareholders—and if those shareholder-owners want to support that mission—so be it. But I balk at the proposition that a company's "stakeholders" (a term often used by collectivists to justify unreasonable demands) should be allowed to control the property of the shareholders. It seems Mackey's philosophy is more accurately described by Karl Marx: "From each according to his ability" (the shareholders surrender money and assets); "to each according to his needs" (the charities, social interest groups, and environmentalists get what they want). That's not free market capitalism.

Then there is the arrogant proposition that if other corporations would simply emulate the higher corporate life form defined by Whole Foods, the world would be better off. After all, Mackey says corporations are viewed as "selfish, greedy, and uncaring." I, for one, consider free market capitalism to be a high calling, even without the infusion of altruism practiced by Whole Foods.

If one goes beyond the sensationalistic journalism surrounding the Enron-like debacles, one discovers that only about 10 to 20 public corporations have been justifiably accused of serious wrongdoing. That's about 0.1 percent of America's 17,500 public companies. What's the failure rate of the publications that demean business? (Consider the *New York Times* scandal involving manufactured stories.) What's the percentage of U.S. presidents who have been forced or almost forced from office? (It's 10 times higher than the failure rate of corporations.) What percentage of our congressmen have spent time in jail? The fact is that despite some well-publicized failures, most corporations are run with the highest ethical standards—and the public knows it. Public opinion polls demonstrate that fact by routinely ranking businessmen above journalists and politicians in esteem.

I am proud of what the semiconductor industry does—relentlessly cutting the cost of a transistor from \$3 in 1960 to *three-millionths* of a dollar today. Mackey would be keeping his business records with hordes of accountants on paper ledgers if our industry didn't exist. He would have to charge his poorest customers more for their food, pay his valued employees less, and cut his philanthropy programs if the semiconductor industry had not focused so relentlessly on increasing its profits, cutting his costs in the process. Of course, if the U.S. semiconductor industry had been less cost-competitive due to its own philanthropy, the food industry simply would have bought cheaper computers made from Japanese and Korean silicon chips (which happened anyway). Layoffs in the nonunion semiconductor industry were actually good news to Whole Foods' unionized grocery store clerks. Where was Mackey's sense of altruism when unemployed semiconductor workers needed it? Of course, that rhetorical question is foolish, since he did exactly the right thing by ruthlessly reducing his recordkeeping costs so as to maximize his profits.

I am proud to be a free market capitalist. And I resent the fact that Mackey's philosophy demeans me as an egocentric child because I have refused on moral grounds to embrace the philosophies of collectivism and altruism that have caused so much human misery, however tempting the sales pitch for them sounds.

> *"It's clear that one reason those on the left have embraced [corporate social responsibility] is that they are having such a hard time achieving their aims through representative democracy."*

# A Left-Wing Agenda Drives the Movement for Corporate Social Responsibility

*James K. Glassman*

*In this viewpoint James K. Glassman, a resident scholar at the American Enterprise Institute, argues that the corporate social responsibility movement is an attempt to divert business from its proper aim, of making a profit for shareholders. In fact, by increasing wealth and prosperity generally, capitalism and profit-oriented businesses are already society's most powerful forces for positive social change.*

As you read, consider the following questions:

1. What is the "new role and purpose" that corporate social responsibility assigns to businesses, according to the author?

James K. Glassman, "Corporate Social Responsibility," *American Enterprise Online*, January-February 2006. Reproduced with permission of The American Enterprise, a national magazine of Politics, Business, and Culture (TAEmag.com).

2. The author argues that free market capitalism makes the world a better place by doing one thing. What is it?

3. The author mentions an organization, Business for Social Responsibility, several times. Why is he critical of this organization?

"Few trends could so thoroughly undermine the very foundations of our free society," wrote [economist] Milton Friedman 43 years ago, "as the acceptance by corporate officials of a social responsibility other than to make as much money for their stockholders as possible." Wow! Now there's a refreshing opinion in a world where CEOs pander to the aging radicals who run the increasingly powerful anti-capitalist entities called non-governmental organizations (NGOs).

In recent years, many CEOs have flocked to support something called "corporate social responsibility," or CSR. (And who could be against that?) In November [2005], for example, Business for Social Responsibility—an organization that includes some of the world's biggest companies, from ABB to Walt Disney—attracted more than 1,000 people to its annual meeting in [Washington,] D.C. World Bank president Paul Wolfowitz gave the keynote address.

While CSR seems unexceptional, it actually "assigns to businesses a new role and purpose," notes economist David Henderson in his 2001 book, *Misguided Virtue*. Under a CSR regime, businesses are supposed to embrace "corporate citizenship" and "run their affairs in close conjunction with an array of different 'stakeholders,' so as to promote the goal of 'sustainable development.'" Economics, social life, and environmental desires are all part of a "triple bottom line" to which businesses must adhere.

"CSR advocates maintain that businesses should assume the major role in making the world a better place," writes Randall Frost. Friedman disagrees. "This is a fundamentally subversive doctrine," he says in *Capitalism and Freedom*. "If

## A Pro CSR Concensus Is Misguided

I believe this pro CSR [corporate social responsibility] concensus is misguided for two related reasons. Reason number one is that the doctrine rests on a distorted view of the modern world. CSR advocates typically maintain the world is in a bad way and getting worse. They paint a picture of growing environmental deterioration and threats together with widespread and increasing inequality social exclusion and injustice. . . .

My second reason for questioning CSR is that putting it into effect will make people poorer. Within businesses its adoption will almost certainly bring higher costs, managers have to take account of new goals and concerns and involve themselves in new process of consultation with stakeholders.

*David Henderson,*
*"The Case Against Corporate Social Responsibility,"*
*December 12, 2001. www.abc.net.au.*

businessmen do have a social responsibility other than making maximum profits for stockholders, how are they to know what it is?"

That's a job for the political process. It's clear that one reason those on the left have embraced CSR is that they are having such a hard time achieving their aims through representative democracy. Environmental and social radicals have built NGOs that acquire power by working closely with kindred spirits in the media to intimidate businesses.

It often works. Henderson quotes Sir Mark Moody-Stuart of Shell Oil: "Because we, too, are concerned at the requirement to address those in poverty who are excluded from the

benefits that many of us share in the global economy, we share the objective of the recent demonstrators in Seattle, Davos, and Prague."

## The Creativity of Market Capitalism

In truth, the best antidote to poverty is economic growth, and the best system for solving financial, social, and physical ills is competitive free-market capitalism. In the atmosphere of creative destruction that market competition creates, corporations have their hands full doing the one job that is required and expected of them—making profits that keep them in business. Certainly, businesses must obey the law, and individual executives must act morally, guided, in most cases, by religion. But the way to "make the world a better place" is to increase financial returns to shareholders.

Groups like Business for Social Responsibility, and the labor and environmental organizations that support CSR, want to yoke business into shortening working hours, fighting global warming, and promoting the interests of women and minorities. The CSR agenda is left-wing, but it's propped up with phrases (like "sustainable development") that seem sensible. The result: CSR gets a free ride because, as *The Economist* put it, "The opponents never turned up."

But that's changing. In an article titled "CSR in the Cross-Hairs," *Business Ethics* magazine reports (in their case with alarm) that, "A broad counterattack against corporate reform is growing." One reason is the backlash against Cal-PERS, the California public employee retirement system that seemed to be putting a social agenda ahead of maximizing the investment that will pay the future pensions of its members. Henderson's book has had an impact, as has the work of Steve Milloy, who launched "CSR Watch" and put on a counter-conference at the same time and in the same hotel as Business for Social Responsibility.

The constant pandering of many of today's business leaders exposes a sad truth: They are embarrassed about what they do for a living. But, as Henderson said in a speech in 2005, "There is no need to apologize for capitalism, nor for profit-oriented business enterprises." They are our society's most powerful forces for progress, the elimination of poverty and illness, and for making people happier. Can CSR do that?

> "More and more people—from institutional investors and fiduciaries to individual investors to stakeholders—are demanding specific, in-depth information about the performance of public companies on social and environmental issues."

# The Corporate Social Responsibility Movement Responds to Real Demand for Increased Accountability

*Peter Kinder*

*Peter Kinder, president of KLD Analytics, an independent investment research firm, argues in this viewpoint that companies must come to terms with increased scrutiny by investors and the demand by investors that companies conduct themselves in socially responsible ways. Investors may be motivated by a variety of different concerns. Whatever their concerns, he says, they take very seriously their need for trustworthy information on which to base their investment decisions.*

Peter Kinder, "Investors and Public Want Corporate Accountability More Than Ever. So Why Is It Under Attack?" *Ethical Corporation*, June 10, 2005. Reproduced by permission.

As you read, consider the following questions:

1. Who are some of critics of the corporate social responsibility movement who are mentioned in this viewpoint?
2. What is "the business case" for corporate social responsibility, as presented in this viewpoint?
3. The author cites Chiquita Brands International as one company that takes corporate social responsibility seriously. What has the company done to demonstrate its social concerns and commitments?

The list of CEOs under scrutiny, either for wrongdoing or poor job performance, continues to grow. From former WorldCom CEO Bernie Ebbers to L. Dennis Kozlowski, former CEO of Tyco International Ltd., to HealthSouth Corp.'s founder and former CEO Richard M. Scrushy, the list of convicted or alleged "wrong-doers" is ever expanding.

On the "failure to perform" side of the list are CEOs—Michael Eisner, CEO of The Walt Disney Company, who steps down in September 2005; Carly Fiorina, former CEO of HP who recently resigned under board pressure; and Harry Stonecipher, former Boeing CEO whose extramarital affair with a female employee violated company ethics policies—whose boards of directors recently have exercised their fiduciary responsibility to hold top executives accountable.

Given the increased scrutiny of public companies by law enforcement agencies and shareholders, one would expect business leaders to embrace the concept of corporate social responsibility (CSR)—"the recognition by corporations that their actions must take into account the needs and ethical standards of society" as central to good corporate governance. Yet, the first quarter of 2005 witnessed a barrage of attacks on corporate social responsibility by business leaders and organizations.

In January [2005], Steve Forbes wrote an editorial critical of CSR in the *Financial Post*. Then, *The Economist* produced a

## The Future of CSR

Corporate Social Responsibility (CSR) is an issue that is working its way into many policy debates and corporate agendas. . . .

A recent survey by PricewaterhouseCoopers of 140 chief executives of U.S.-based multinational companies found that 85 per cent of them believe that sustainable development will be even more important to their business model in five years than it is today.

*International Institute for Sustainable Development,*
*"ISO 26000 (CSR Guidance)," 2008. www.iisd.org.*

negative cover story and 10,000-word "survey." In addition, Arthur Laffer and the Competitive Enterprise Institute attacked CSR's effects on corporate profits.

At a March 2005 gathering of corporate executives in Boston, Nestle CEO and Chairman-elect Peter Brabeck-Letmathe argued, "What the hell have we taken away from society by being a successful company that employs people? Companies should only pursue charitable endeavors with an underlying intention of making money for investors."

Weyerhaeuser's [one of the largest pulp and paper companies in the world] management eliminated shareholder questions at their AGM [annual general meeting] and physically removed owners who objected. In April, a lead Sunday business section story in the *New York Times* was headlined, "Managers to Owners: Shut Up."

## The Case for CSR

What to make of this? Many corporate executives fundamentally misunderstand the concept of corporate social responsibility.

KPMG's International Chairman Michael Rake told the World Economic Forum, "The first thing people need to understand around corporate social responsibility is that the business case is very strong. If you look at any survey, all other things being equal (such as price and quality), the consumer will buy from the company that has a responsible attitude towards its community. In recruitment, people want to work for a company with a responsible social attitude."

CSR is fundamentally about business holding themselves accountable for their impact on people and the planet. It is a comprehensive approach that a corporation takes to meet or exceed stakeholder expectations beyond measures of revenue, profit, and legal obligations. It is not about philanthropy. It is not about anyone's—shareholder, stakeholder, or manager—disdain for profit.

Many companies, too, take CSR seriously and are putting resources behind it. Chiquita Brands International Inc. announced earlier this year the appointment of a corporate responsibility officer who will "oversee Chiquita's adherence to leading environmental, social and ethical standards and the measurement, verification and reporting of the company's performance in those areas." According to Chiquita's CEO Fernando Aguirre, the company wants to "ensure that corporate responsibility continues to be woven into every major decision we make as a company."

## Response to Critics

What critics fear about CSR is increased scrutiny and accountability. Thus, CSR exposes them to reputational, financial, and legal risks. The response to critics of CSR lies in a simple fact: the demand from shareholders and the public is growing (the Social Investment Forum says over $2 trillion is invested under social mandates).

More and more people—from institutional investors and fiduciaries to individual investors to stakeholders—are de-

manding specific, in-depth information about the performance of public companies on social and environmental issues.

Some investors simply want to invest based on their values, whether those lean for or against specific social or environmental issues. They don't want gun manufacturers in their portfolios. Faith-based institutions often want to ensure that their investment portfolios do not include so-called "vice" stocks—companies with operations, holdings, or investments in alcohol, tobacco, gambling, or adult entertainment. Other investors believe that companies with good CSR track records make better long-term investments.

Regardless of their motivations, investors want information they can trust about public companies. The recent wave of bad behavior by corporate CEOs has eroded their trust. As investors increase their expectations for greater corporate social responsibility and demand greater access to information about the institutions they own, managers must learn to adapt to new market conditions. Isn't that a key measure of success with which everyone can agree?

> "One way of looking at CSR [corporate social responsibility] is that it is part of what businesses need to do to keep up with (or, if possible, stay slightly ahead of) society's fast-changing expectations. It is an aspect of taking care of a company's reputation, managing its risks, and gaining a competitive edge."

# Corporate Social Responsibility Is an Enlightened Response to the Pressures of Globalization

## The Economist

*This viewpoint, first printed as an editorial in* The Economist *magazine, argues that because information spreads so quickly in the era of global markets, corporate social responsibility (CSR) has become an essential part of doing business. The author contends that the extraordinary wealth creation of recent years has produced a new entrepreneurial model for social responsibility. In a few cutting-edge companies, CSR is championed from the top down, rather than being an activity of the corporate commu-*

*nications office. The author further notes that well-run companies that have a strong commitment to corporate social responsibility are likely to experience commercial success, and over time, the practice of corporate social responsibility will help to sustain profits for shareholders. The Economist is a newspaper that focuses on international politics and business news.*

As you read, consider the following questions:

1. What are some of the things the author cites as evidence of widespread interest in corporate social responsibility?
2. Why does the author say that within companies, corporate social responsibility initiatives could be especially vulnerable to the effects of an economic recession?
3. According to this viewpoint, what are some of the risks of being a corporate social responsibility leader? Why might it be better to be "number two or number three" on corporate social responsibility, rather than to be considered a leader?

The CSR [corporate social responsibility] industry, as we have seen, is in rude health. Company after company has been shaken into adopting a CSR policy: it is almost unthinkable today for a big global corporation to be without one. Climate change has added further impetus. Investors are taking an ever greater interest. New and surprising sorts of cooperation are springing up: with NGOs [non-governmental organizations], with competitors, with other companies. The message is moving across supply chains and spreading around the world.

What has helped to make all this possible is globalisation—which has also been responsible for much of the general wealth-creation through which companies, let it not be forgotten, make their main contribution to society. A sudden bout of protectionism, which is by no means out of the question, could put it at risk. So activists who press for various

forms of protection should be careful what they wish for. An economic recession would also be bad news for the CSR industry, parts of which might be seen as a luxury companies could live without.

But assuming that corporate goodness continues to flourish, how will things evolve? The next wave, some believe, will be one of disruptive innovation, featuring a new breed of "social entrepreneur" that will take over from the established big companies as the driving force. Mr [Marc] Benioff of salesforce.com reckons that social entrepreneurs have "cracked the code" of the next generation of corporate responsibility: it will be for-profit and self-sustaining. Mr Benioff himself plumbed philanthropy into his company right from the start by committing 1% of equity, profits and employees' time as a contribution to the community.

## A World of New Wealth

The extraordinary wealth-creation of recent years has produced a large number of extremely rich people, many of them from the software and finance industries, who are interested in a new kind of philanthropy: a smart, capitalist kind. It involves using money for maximum impact by investing in potentially disruptive technologies (in the environmental field, for example) and in social enterprises that can be scaled up as required.

This kind of enterprise has several advantages over established big business. It has focus, rather than being a sideline, as CSR often is for large companies. It involves people who are using their own money and are interested in measurable results: "real good" not "feelgood". It brings financial rigour as well as an appetite for risk, and it can teach the big companies a thing or two about how to measure the success of social investments.

The sums involved are not trivial. That is partly thanks to Bill Gates, who in June [2008] will leave his full-time job at

Microsoft to work at his fabulously rich charitable foundation. This will aim to be giving away $3 billion a year by 2009, more than any other foundation anywhere. Money also pours in through innovative charities such as Absolute Return for Kids in London, which invests donors' money with entrepreneurs on the ground in developing countries.

The entrepreneurial model of tackling social and environmental problems is likely to stir up the CSR world. It may over time produce transformative technologies and creative new business models. But for now it is still big businesses that can make a difference. Large companies will find ways of working with—and sometimes absorbing—successful social ventures. In the next few years CSR will be mainly about "how large corporations steer a sustainable growth strategy in a very complex environment", as Jane Nelson of Harvard University puts it. . . .

## Few Leaders, Many Laggards

Some companies are doing interesting things, both to manage their risks and to exploit opportunities. But such examples are relatively scarce: the same few familiar names pop up again and again. Like most industries, the corporate-responsibility business has a handful of leaders, a large number of followers and many laggards.

You can recognise the leaders partly from the way they are grappling with particularly tricky issues, such as how to apply codes of practice across global supply chains or how best to convey accurate environmental information on product labels. The leaders typically have a committed CEO who champions the policy, a chief officer for corporate responsibility—or sustainability or whatever—who reports to the boss, and a cross-functional board committee to ensure that strategy is coordinated throughout the company. Non-financial measures of progress often play an important part in the overall assess-

## Corporate Social Responsibility Makes Sense

Your business doesn't exist in isolation, simply as a way of making money. Your employees depend on your business. Customers, suppliers and the local community are all affected by you and what you do. Your products, and the way you make them, have an impact on the environment.

Corporate social responsibility (CSR) takes all this into account. It isn't about being "right on", or mounting an expensive publicity exercise. It simply means taking a responsible attitude and following simple principles that apply whatever the size of your business.

*BusinessLink, "Corporate Social Responsibility," 2008.*
*www.businesslink.gov.uk.*

ment of the company's performance. These are companies, in short, that are seeking to "embed" CSR in the business.

Not every company can be a leader, nor should they all want to be. Being a high-profile early enthusiast carries the risk of overpromising. First-mover advantage soon passes. After a while, for example, everybody turns green, and the winners are the companies with the best execution. One large consultancy advises its big clients to be number two or three on corporate responsibility rather than number one. Thoughtful firms may pick and choose across the spectrum of CSR activities where to be ahead and where merely to comply with the rules.

The followers in the CSR industry are many. By now they probably produce a glossy report which lists numerous worthy activities—too many, in fact, when it would be better to con-

centrate on those that really work and benefit the business. The companies concerned may have little idea whether their carbon-offset scheme is effective or their ethical-purchasing plan costs jobs. Their real motive is public relations, and the telltale sign is that the person responsible for CSR sits in the corporate-communications department.

And the laggards? There are two types. Companies in the first group have simply failed to pay much attention to CSR; they risk being attacked as "late adopters". Those in the second group, more cynically, think they can afford to ignore CSR, at least for now. Perhaps they are in an industry with a low profile, or operate in countries where scrutiny is minimal. They do not mind being viewed as freeloaders by competitors who spend time and money on trying to be good corporate citizens. Over time, though, this could also be risky if they find themselves subject to greater scrutiny or miss out on opportunities.

## Doing What Comes Naturally

One way of looking at CSR is that it is part of what businesses need to do to keep up with (or, if possible, stay slightly ahead of) society's fast-changing expectations. It is an aspect of taking care of a company's reputation, managing its risks and gaining a competitive edge. This is what good managers ought to do anyway. Doing it well may simply involve a clearer focus and greater effort than in the past, because information now spreads much more quickly and companies feel the heat.

So paying attention to CSR can amount to enlightened self-interest, something that over time will help to sustain profits for shareholders. The truly responsible business never loses sight of the commercial imperative. It is, after all, by staying in business and providing products and services people want that firms do most good. If ignoring CSR is risky, ignoring what makes business sense is a certain route to failure.

It is the interaction between a company's principles and its commercial competence that shapes the kind of business it will be. A company that is weak on both values and commercial competence is simply a bad business. One that has strong values but is badly run, without proper attention to translating values into profits, will plainly not do well. In contrast, a company that is highly competent commercially but does not bother with corporate responsibility may work just fine, but it could also prove increasingly risky. Lastly, a combination of a strong commitment to CSR and strong commercial competence gives a good chance of success.

If it is nothing more than good business practice, is there any point in singling out corporate social responsibility as something distinctive? Strangely, perhaps there is, at least for now. If it helps businesses look outwards more than they otherwise would and to think imaginatively about the risks and opportunities they face, it is probably worth doing. This is why some financial analysts think that looking at the quality of a company's CSR policy may be a useful pointer to the quality of its management more generally.

True, much of what is done in the name of CSR is nothing of the sort. It often amounts to little more than the PR [public relations] department sending its own messages to the outside world. Yet in a growing number of companies CSR goes deeper than that and comes closer to being "embedded" in the business, influencing decisions on everything from sourcing to strategy. These may also be the places where talented people will most want to work.

The more this happens, ironically, the more the days of CSR may start to seem numbered. In time it will simply be the way business is done in the 21st century. "My job is to design myself out of a job," says one company's head of corporate responsibility.

For the moment, though, chief sustainability officers and their ilk [kind] remain in high demand. No doubt there will

also be growing opportunities for ones that speak Mandarin or Hindi as the fashion for corporate social responsibility spreads around the world. And it will be quite a while yet before they all become redundant.

"*Although CSR [corporate social responsibility] advocates portray a profit-centric corporation as socially irresponsible, the opposite is true. A profit-centric firm provides the optimal amount of socially responsible behavior.*"

# Corporate Social Responsibility Should Be Driven by Consumers and Markets

*Andrew C. Coors and Wayne Winegarden*

*Andrew C. Coors, a senior manager for Qualcomm and formerly employed by Laffer Associates, joins Wayne Winegarden of Sterling International in arguing in this viewpoint that companies behave in socially responsible ways when they provide goods and services that consumers want to buy. In competitive markets, the balancing of supply and demand maximizes social welfare. Social change should begin with a change in consumer's preferences.*

Andrew C. Coors and Wayne Winegarden, "Corporate Social Responsibility—Or Good Advertising?" *Regulation*, Spring 2005, pp. 10–11. Republished with permission of The Cato Institute, conveyed through Copyright Clearance Center, Inc.

As you read, consider the following questions:

1. What is the original purpose of any company, according to the authors of this viewpoint?

2. The authors compare two hypothetical companies, identical except that one engages in "socially responsible behaviors." Why do they say that the socially responsible company will eventually fail?

3. Do you agree with the authors that a company's decision to pursue corporate social responsibility is essentially a marketing decision?

In the United States, Corporate Managers are fiduciary agents for a firm's owners—the shareholders. Those managers should act in the interest of the shareholders by maximizing the returns of the company. Despite that responsibility to the owners, some people argue that a company should be responsible to a much more broadly defined group: stakeholders—those people who are affected by a firm's behavior. The problem with this, the corporate social responsibility (CSR) perspective, is that a company focused solely on pleasing all stakeholders will go out of business.

Ultimately, the corporation is only a reflection of consumers' demands and priorities; true social change necessarily involves changes in consumers' demands. Voluntary CSR is really nothing more than corporate advertising that makes consumers aware of new products with features for which they are willing to pay. Although CSR advocates portray a profit-centric corporation as socially irresponsible, the opposite is true. A profit-centric firm provides the optimal amount of socially responsible behavior.

## What Is CSR?

The ethic of corporate social responsibility has been described as "the alignment of business operations with social values. CSR consists of integrating the interest of stakeholders—all of

those affected by a company's conduct—into the company's business policies and actions." Fundamentally, socially responsible behavior internalizes all external consequences of an action, both its costs and benefits.

But there is a problem with this definition. What should a company value in its pursuit of social responsibility? Should it attempt to minimize the negative impacts of its business activity, or maximize its positive impacts, or find some optimal combination of positive and negative impacts? And how much do various stakeholders' preferences matter? Do the opinions of environmentalists count more than those of labor activists? Or shareholders? Or consumers?

Those questions can become so overwhelming and convoluted that they quickly distract a company from its original purpose—to provide profits to shareholders while supplying consumers with goods and services that add tangible benefits to their lives. Companies provide consumers with goods and services that they prefer enough to forgo other consumption. If consumers are willing to pay a premium for more socially responsible production, however that is defined, then businesses would be actively pursuing those methods of production without any new organizational framework besides simple creative profit maximization.

The fact that the market gives us precisely what we ask of it is difficult for many CSR advocates to believe. A business's methods of production and the products it provides are mirrors that reflect individuals' preferences and economic trade-offs given a budget constraint. For example, gasoline stations would begin selling biomass fuel tomorrow if consumers were willing to pay the premium necessary to make that venture profitable; but, in general, consumers are not yet willing to make that monetary sacrifice. Sure, there is discontent with the pollution that stems from our combustion-based economy, but consumers do not seem to be eager to pay more than current gasoline prices to relieve their discontent.

The economic dance of supply and demand works to maximize social welfare, but externalities such as pollution are sometimes produced in the supply process. To combat those externalities, government sometimes (arguably too frequently) intervenes in the private market, implementing incentives and disincentives in attempts to change consumer or supplier behavior. The government can tax a product, thereby manipulating the market to address the externalities produced. In those cases, the government attempts to force firms to act in a socially responsible manner by changing the equilibrium conditions of the market. The government has the ability to pass the cost of an externality onto consumers through "Pigouvian taxes." However, to the demise of CSR theory, firms cannot unilaterally pass externality costs downward onto consumers just by increasing the price. Any company that attempts to add back the externality's costs without a signal from the government or consumers will be punished by investors.

## The Cost of Risking Profits

Take two firms producing an interchangeable and indistinguishable commodity. One company strictly tries to maximize profits, but the other engages in socially responsible behaviors such as charitable donations. That social responsibility (if not demanded by consumers) will come at the cost of profits. The profit-maximizing company will be able to reinvest and grow more rapidly than the socially responsible competitor. The profit-maximizing company will gain market share as it takes advantage of economies of scale, undercutting its competition. Eventually, the "socially responsible" company will fail. The result: the socially conscious management team and its employees are out of work and on the unemployment rolls, while consumers are worse off because there is less competition (and possibly higher prices) in the marketplace. Everyone is worse off because there is less economic activity.

## Tips for a Successful Corporate Social Responsibility Marketing Campaign

- Honesty breeds customer loyalty. Create CSR [corporate social responsibility] marketing campaigns based in truth and on the value your company provides to the marketplace. Fireman's Fund, a property casualty insurer, has launched several initiatives to support firefighters and create safer communities.

- Balance creativity with on-target messaging. Creativity counts, but simplicity works too and can be easier to implement. For years, McDonald's has marketed anti-litter initiatives.

- Forging alliances strengthens outreach. A partnership between two seemingly unlikely parties can be just the ticket to CSR success. Allstate worked with the National Council of La Raza, an organization advocating Hispanic civil rights, to create a program geared towards empowering youth leadership.

*BurrellesLuce,*
*"Hitting the Right Note:*
*Best Practices for Corporate Social Responsibility Marketing,"*
*July 2007. www.burrellesluce.com.*

The optimal solution would have been for both firms to compete strictly based on profit maximization, and then allow consumers, stockholders, and employees to decide whether they want to donate some of their cost savings, profits, or wages to socially responsible activities. Each person would weigh the costs and benefits individually and come up with an appropriate dollar amount to contribute. In this scenario, people remain employed, the economic growth rate is higher, more jobs are created, consumers have more choices, there is

more competition in the marketplace, and everyone enjoys lower prices. In addition, leaving the decision of charitable donations to individuals results in a superior allocation of funds. It is the consumer that should bear the burden of a conscience, not the corporation.

## CSR That Makes Sense

Companies logically pursue any CSR activity that yields positive returns after all costs are considered. The only reason for a firm not to engage in a socially responsible activity is because consumers are not willing to pay extra for the additional cost. The socially responsible activity must be more costly than other methods of production, otherwise companies would do it proactively to profit maximize. Engaging in an unprofitable corporate responsible action would either lower company profits, raise prices, lower wages, lower the number of employees hired, or a combination of all four. Interestingly (but not surprisingly), those four outcomes also occur when a tax is levied on a firm.

When a corporation voluntarily engages in socially responsible activity, it does so to advertise its behavior, differentiate its product, increase market share, and boost profits. For example, enter any Starbucks and you are surrounded by advertisements explaining how socially conscious Starbucks is. BP is now "Beyond Petroleum" in an attempt to persuade consumers that the firm is not "Big Oil." The list goes on and on, begging the question, is there a difference between traditional advertising and advertising a company's socially responsible behavior? Both are attempts to increase sales and profits.

Of course, a company would not employ advertising unless the advertising yields the company additional revenue, otherwise it would just be throwing away money. Would this logic not hold for CSR too? Just because the advertising comes in the form of social responsibility, it does not make it any

less like advertising. A firm would no sooner make an anonymous donation to a charity than it would buy 30 seconds of silence on the radio.

## Tailoring CSR to Consumer Preferences

The corporate decision about whether to pursue CSR can be approached by management just like a marketing decision—with cost/benefit analysis. If a company advertises its corporate social responsibility as a substitute for traditional advertising, the implication is that social responsibility follows from a corporation's desire to influence consumer preferences. It does not mean that the firm's corporate behavior has somehow been "reshaped" as the CSR literature would have you believe; the firm is still trying to maximize profits, and it believes it will do so by adopting (and advertising) the CSR ethic.

Thus, when consumers' preferences change, companies' behaviors change. Those corporations that do not follow such rules fail to do so at their own peril. If enough consumers change their preferences to purchase more socially responsible corporate products, then companies will meet that demand because they are continually trying to maximize profits. But let us be perfectly clear, in this dance between consumers and corporations, it is the consumers who lead.

So can social responsibility exist? Sure. We would be the last to say that a firm should not act in a reasonable manner. But activists and managers must realize that the path to social responsibility needs to rely on the carrot and stick of consumers' actions. If a firm wants to articulate change in a consumer's demand function to rationalize CSR activities, then the firm must advertise. And if a company is engaging in CSR activities, it had better be using those activities to garner customers and increase profits, or else management is not fulfilling its duties.

# Periodical Bibliography

*The following articles have been selected to supplement the diverse views presented in this chapter.*

David Altschul
"Ebenezer Brand, and Other Stories: Profit Is Good. Creating Shareholder Value Is Good. But When Consumers Suspect That the Only Thing a Brand Cares About Is Money, We Have What's Called the Scrooge Effect," *Brandweek*, June 16, 2008.

Kelly Bronk
"The Do-Good Disconnect; More MBA Students Are Interested in Social Responsibility, But a Well-Paying Job Is More Important, According to a New Study," April 22, 2008. www.businessweek.com.

Jo Causon
"Burning Career Issues," *Personnel Today*, September 6, 2008.

*The Economist*
"Strange Bedfellows; Companies as Activists," May 24, 2008.

Allison Hall
"Give Back Get Raves," *Financial & Insurance Meetings*, September 1, 2008.

Mike Hofan
"The Best Cause of All: U.S. Companies Are by Far Bigger Givers than Their Global Counterparts. Yet They're Not Particularly Interested in Doing Good. What Gives?" *Inc.*, June 2008.

Matthew Kirdahy
"Big Business Gives Back," June 12, 2008. www.forbes.com.

Adam Smith
"Caring Capitalists," *Time International*, June 23, 2008.

Rebecca Tonn
"Corporate Social Responsibility: Profitable, Conscionable," *Colorado Springs Business Journal*, June 6, 2008.

OPPOSING
VIEWPOINTS®
SERIES

CHAPTER 2

# How Have Corporations Been Impacted by Environmental Concerns?

# Chapter Preface

BP, one of the world's largest producers of oil and gas, has been an active participant in the conversation about how to reverse climate change. In 1996, BP resigned from the Global Climate Coalition, an industry group that had challenged the science of global warming and actively opposed the progress of the Kyoto Treaty to reduce worldwide consumption of greenhouse gases. Lord John Browne, CEO of BP at that time, explained that "the time to consider the policy dimensions of climate change is not when the link between greenhouse gases and climate change is conclusively proven, but when the possibility cannot be discounted and is taken seriously by the society of which we are part." In the years since, BP has attempted to reshape itself as an enlightened and responsible corporation, at the forefront of efforts to develop clean energy alternatives. It has invested in wind and solar power, and in the development of biofuels such as cellulosic ethanol that can provide a cleaner alternative to fossil fuels. It has also mounted a high-profile green marketing campaign that portrays the company as "Beyond Petroleum."

The BP Web site outlines the company's support of actions to limit greenhouse gas emissions, and other efforts to combat climate change. These include a sustainable timetable for the reduction of greenhouse gas emissions, policy and regulatory interventions that support economic progress and provide energy security through the development of new energy technologies, the use of emission caps and emissions trading to help companies adapt to a carbon-constrained world, incentives for the development of renewable energy sources, and recognition of the continuing place of fossil fuels in the world's energy economy. "We see our . . . role as pursuing efficiency in our own operations," the BP Web site says, "creating lower carbon products for customers and contributing to an informed debate."

Paradoxically, BP's efforts to create a more socially responsible profile for itself have made it a target of criticism from environmental groups who have portrayed the company's clean energy efforts as insincere. BP has been accused of "greenwashing"—of co-opting the language and imagery of the environmental movement to differentiate itself in a market in which, environmentally speaking, perhaps it does not differ that much from its oil and gas competitors. Some critics claim that BP spends more promoting its clean energy image than it does developing clean energy technologies. In a 2006 article, "Hope vs. Hype: Is Corporate Do-Goodery for Real?" environmental writer Bill McKibben pointed out that BP's revenues from alternative energy sources are actually quite small, amounting to "one-sixth of 1 percent," of more than $285 billion in sales. A writer for *Fortune* magazine, taking a different turn on the same facts, ridiculed BP's green marketing campaign as an odd way to promote a company that in fact makes billions of dollars selling oil and gas. "If the world's second-largest oil company is beyond petroleum, *Fortune* is beyond words," she wrote.

SourceWatch, an organization that monitors and documents activities of public relations firms, has suggested that BP's green marketing campaign created expectations that the company has simply been unable to meet.

The case of BP illustrates the difficult social and economic context in which companies must operate in an era of increasing sensitivity to environmental concerns. How have corporations been impacted by concerns about the environment? Is it possible to run a profitable business while addressing environmental concerns in a responsible way? How can corporate leaders prepare themselves and their organizations to better respond to environmental challenges? These are some of the questions that are addressed in the viewpoints of this chapter.

> *"It is unsurprising that large, multinational companies seek ways of 'avoiding criticism from the public and from the customers.' That is good business practice. The interesting wrinkle . . . is that they would do this at a cost in profit and enterprise."*

# Green Initiatives Are Not Always Good for Business or the Environment

*Nick Schultz*

*In this viewpoint Nick Schultz, editor in chief of* The American *magazine, argues that the environmental sensitivities of large multinational corporations, which make little sense from an economic standpoint, often aren't of much benefit for the environment either. In evaluating the costs and the promises of green initiatives, businesses should think hard about the wisdom of sacrificing profits for outcomes that aren't of real benefit to the environment.*

Nick Schultz, "The Greening of Capitalism," American Enterprise Institute for Public Policy Research, July 2, 2007. Reproduced by permission.

As you read, consider the following questions:

1. The author quotes John Maynard Keynes, who says that large business organizations tend to socialize themselves over time. What kinds of things does a business do to socialize itself, according to Keynes?

2. How is corporate social responsibility defined in this article?

3. How, according to the author, can corporate social responsibility result in harm to the environment?

After the Paris Peace Conference in 1919, the great British economist John Maynard Keynes returned to Cambridge for most of the next twenty years to write and teach. It was an extraordinarily fruitful period for him. It was there that he penned his most famous work, *The General Theory of Employment, Interest, and Money*, published in 1936. But prior to publishing his *General Theory*, Keynes produced several other smaller and lesser-known volumes that helped him develop his famous opus. Among these was an essay entitled "The End of Laissez-Faire," based on lectures he had delivered in Oxford and Berlin. Looking back on it today, that short work is striking for its prescience. Keynes notes that "one of the most interesting and unnoticed developments of recent decades has been the tendency of big enterprise to socialize itself." He continues:

> A point arrives in the growth of a big institution . . . at which the owners of the capital, i.e. the shareholders, are almost entirely dissociated from the management, with the result that the direct personal interest of the latter in the making of great profit becomes quite secondary. When this stage is reached, the general stability and reputation of the institution are more considered by the management than the maximum of profit for the shareholders. The shareholders must be satisfied by conventionally adequate dividends; but once this is secured, the direct interest of the management

often consists in avoiding criticism from the public and from the customers of the concern. . . . They are, as time goes on, socializing themselves.

Keynes was allied with the anti-conservative Bloomsbury set and a critic of the then-emerging highly dynamic industrial capitalism that was based upon an unapologetic pursuit of profit. For Keynes the tendency of large firms towards socialization was in some significant ways a good thing—not unambiguously good, but beneficent in the long run.

## The Beginnings of the Corporate Social Responsibility Movement

From our vantage point today, it is unsurprising that large, multinational companies seek ways of "avoiding criticism from the public and from the customers." That is good business practice. The interesting wrinkle that Keynes noted, and the one that should concern us today, is that they would do this at a cost in profit and enterprise. And in this Keynes foreshadowed what has come to be known as the Corporate Social Responsibility (CSR) movement.

The premises of CSR are that corporate entities, particularly large and powerful ones, have responsibilities that extend beyond ensuring the most desirable returns for their owners, the shareholders. They have obligations to their communities, to the environment, to society (however it is defined), to abstract notions of justice and fairness, and to future generations. Corporate Social Responsibility means firms are obligated, in a sense, to socialize themselves—just as Keynes saw they were already beginning to do.

The embrace of CSR has been swift and firm in American business schools and boardrooms. It is given high priority in the planning and positioning of major business enterprises. Most major corporations have senior executives charged with developing CSR policies for their firms.

The advance of CSR initiatives has also spawned a cottage industry of management consultants who help firms modify their practices and products in a business climate where reputation matters as much as—and sometimes more than—maximizing profit.

*Green to Gold*, the new book from Yale University professors Daniel C. Esty and Andrew S. Winston, is a kind of CSR manual. The authors accept uncritically what Keynes perceived: that the managers of firms of a certain size will go to great lengths to avoid criticism. Their book is designed to help these firms in their efforts.

The present political and cultural climate of opinion places a premium on environmental sensitivity—or at least the appearance of it. Ecological causes are in fashion. "Green is the new black," as *Vanity Fair* magazine recently proclaimed. Or as Esty and Winston put it, there is a "green wave" growing and building momentum through our culture and politics. The consequences for commerce are enormous. The question for the authors is not whether but how, and how quickly, firms become "wave riders" and embrace environmentalism.

## The Politics of CSR

To the extent that business interests and the environment are seen to be in conflict with one another, the environment is winning in the court of public opinion. It is doing so in the court of political opinion as well.

For example, today's Republican Party is widely viewed as the more "pro-business" of the two dominant American political parties. And yet many of the party's stars are quick to demonstrate green sensibilities. California governor Arnold Schwarzenegger has pushed some of the most stringent (some would say fanciful) environmental regulations in the country. Republican Senator and leading presidential aspirant John McCain has lobbied for years for strong global warming regulations. Senator McCain models his political attitudes on

those of Teddy Roosevelt, who pushed Progressive-era environmental and conservation reforms.

It is true that the party's present standard-bearer, President George W. Bush, is widely vilified by green interest groups. But contrary to this perception, President Bush pushed for adoption of alternative energy technologies, particularly wind energy, while serving as governor of Texas. And he is promoting the development of hydrogen technologies and alternative fuel sources, such as switchgrass, devoting considerable sums of federal largesse to those efforts.

None of this is surprising. As countries advance economically and become richer, they become greener and cleaner as well. So even while debates continue over how best to address challenges like global warming, there is nonetheless a thick green thread stitched into today's supposedly "anti-environment" Republican Party. And such attitudes are, of course, even more prominent and significant on the political left. Given this state of affairs, there is a sizeable niche for authors like Esty and Winston to peddle advice on how best to ride the wave.

## The Moral Ambiguities of Green

*Green to Gold* is chockablock with interesting and illuminating examples of firms that adopted green strategies and used them to enhance their reputations and get an edge over competitors. Toyota's commercial success with its Prius hybrid automobile is one example of what the authors term "green to gold" thinking. Toyota anticipated public and political demand, embraced an environmental ethos, and developed products in keeping with that spirit. As Esty and Winston point out, Toyota's decision to "go green" has also done wonders for the company's bottom line, in the form of a popular and brisk-selling automobile.

Some critics have pointed out that the Prius is not as "green" as its image would suggest. For example, the nickel

and other metals required for its battery power system are mined by methods that are far from friendly to the environment. But that point is largely irrelevant from the green-to-gold point of view. For Esty and Winston, the perception that the Prius is eco-friendly is what matters in the marketplace.

As the authors argue, "The logic of corporate environmental stewardship need not stem from a personal belief that caring for the natural world is the right thing to do. If critical stakeholders believe the environment matters, then it's the right thing to do for your business."

If you are a manager at a firm looking to burnish its environmental credentials, this is the book you should buy. If your firm has already committed itself to the trendy belief that it should position itself as a green company, then hire Esty and Winston to advise you. Their book is sensible and pragmatic. Like many management books, it employs a few too many clichés, but in the main, it provides useful information for people looking for advice on how to go green.

But the authors would have done a greater service had they also wrestled more thoughtfully with some of the tough cases that don't fit so tidily into their green-to-gold calculus. Consider a few illustrations.

## Cases That Raise Questions

In the late 1980s, the company Scott Paper, now owned by Kimberly-Clark, sought to operate a eucalyptus plantation and paper mill in Indonesia. A radical environmental group, the Rainforest Action Network, orchestrated a letter-writing effort and threatened a boycott to pressure the firm. The "Stop Scott" campaign paid off and the company backed down. It chose the ostensibly green path. The environment won.

Or did it?

Alissa Stern, coauthor of *The Process of Business/ Environmental Collaborations* pointed out in *The Washington Post* in 2003 that after Scott abandoned its plan, PT Inhutani

## Winning the Battle but Losing the Big Picture

It seemed too clear-cut: A feisty American environmental group stops a big, bad multinational paper company from chopping down an Indonesian rain forest larger than the state of Delaware. Hailing the power of consumer boycotts, the environmental group takes out full-page newspaper ads declaring victory.

That was 14 years and many trees ago. The reality was more complicated then, and has become even more complicated since. The multinational company is gone from Indonesia, but so is a chunk of rain forest it sought to develop. Gone, too, is another swath of rain forest the company had pledged to protect—victim to a state-owned Indonesian company that gladly stepped in. . . .

The main players in this drama were Scott Paper, which wanted pulp for its paper towels, toilet paper and other products, and Rainforest Action Network (RAN), a U.S. environmental group, which organized a letter-writing campaign and threatened a consumer boycott to stop Scott's plans. Today, RAN's Web site still trumpets its success. Under the heading "Your Actions Change the World," it says that as a result of Scott Paper's pullout, "Two million acres of rain forest were saved."

*Alissa J. Stern,*
*"How They Won the Battle and Lost the Rain Forest,"*
The Washington Post, *June 1, 2003.*

II, a state-owned forestry company, took over, looking only for quick production and quick profits with plans to develop

three times as much acreage as Scott would have. PT Inhutani II isn't vulnerable to the same pressures as Scott. It does not sell directly to consumers, so boycotts aren't a bother. And the result has been far worse environmental degradation than Scott would have caused.

"The company has been doing such an efficient job of deforestation," Stern wrote,

> that even Indonesia's not-so-green Ministry of Forestry this year threatened to take back the concession and sell it off piecemeal to small companies. But the practices of small (typically fly-by-night) forestry concerns might be even less environmentally sound than those of PT Inhutani II. Environmental groups will have even less leverage over them, and the government even less control.

Clearly, there are instances when a Western multinational can choose the "green" path, as it did in Scott's case by yielding to environmental pressure groups, and yet the overall outcome will not in fact be environmentally beneficial. What's more, Indonesian businesses and citizens who would have benefited from a relationship with a large company such as Scott Paper—with the resultant technology transfers, knowledge exchanges, and environmental best practice—were denied that opportunity. Scott Paper may have burnished its environmental reputation by its surrender, and faced as it was with a boycott and a pressure campaign, one can sympathize with the company's decision. But Indonesians and their environment are almost certainly worse off.

## Recent Developments

Consider another green-to-gold move, this one involving environmental concerns over biotechnology. A small California company called Ventria Bioscience has developed a promising new gene-splicing technique. This "biopharming" technique takes synthesized human genes that produce the proteins lacto-

ferrin and lysozyme and inserts them in rice. These proteins can fight diarrhea and dehydration and could be extremely beneficial to residents of the developing world where those ailments are major killers of children.

There is at the present time no sound scientific reason to worry about contamination from biopharmed products like those developed by Ventria. There is no serious known risk to human health or the food supply. Nevertheless, environmental pressure groups dislike these agricultural biotechnologies and try to block them by alarming the general public about their safety.

During their development efforts, Ventria hoped to plant the rice in Missouri. And that's when Anheuser-Busch, America's largest rice buyer, stepped in. Anticipating possible public concern over genetically modified rice that might turn up in its beverages, the company threatened to boycott all Missouri rice to block the biotech crop planting. In the end, Ventria was forced to agree not to plant its genetically modified rice any closer than 120 miles from other Missouri rice fields.

The green-to-gold framework outlined by Esty and Winston encourages firms to go green up and down their supply chains and to anticipate public alarm before it emerges. So from that perspective, Anheuser-Busch took a prudent step. And from a commercial standpoint, no one can argue with Anheuser-Busch's decision. Product recalls can be costly and damage reputations. Anheuser-Busch took steps to protect its investments. If I worked for the company, I would probably have advocated the same measure.

But to the extent that safe but unfashionable technologies like Ventria's are delayed due to green ideological concerns, the cost can be measured in life-saving innovations delayed or stymied. So from a wider societal and public health standpoint, it's not clear that the green-to-gold strategy is desirable. At the very least, the picture is more morally nuanced and

complicated than the authors fully appreciate or acknowledge in their book. And to that end, the green-to-gold thesis leaves a series of thorny questions unaddressed.

Keynes was strikingly prophetic eighty years ago when he described the tendency of large enterprises to socialize themselves. And he was pleased with certain aspects of that. But should we be? What of the "waning of enterprise" that Keynes pointed out might come with it? Or the threat to innovation as evidenced in these and other examples? "We are all Keynesians now," Richard Nixon supposedly said. Alas, in this instance, he may have been correct.

> *"Over the past few years ... what's become apparent is that a growing number of companies are looking more intensively at their operations with an eye to using CSR [corporate social responsibility] initiatives to improve their environmental and social track records, as well as the bottom line."*

# Green Initiatives Can Make Firms More Profitable

*John Lorinc*

*John Lorinc, a Toronto-based writer, argues in this viewpoint that companies that have retooled their businesses to be more ecologically sustainable have discovered that their environmentally responsible practices are also financially advantageous. Lorinc cites inefficient energy use and toxic emissions, for example, can turn into significant future expenses; addressing the problems proactively strengthens profitability. In addition to financial savings realized by environmentally responsible operations, companies are discovering that practicing corporate social responsibility (CSR) is good public relations, says Lorinc. The*

John Lorinc, "Good Guys Finish First," *CAmagazine*, May 2008. Reproduced by permission from CA Magazine, published by the Canadian Institute of Chartered Accountants, Toronto.

*largest companies, with the highest public profiles, are pursuing CSR most aggressively, realizing that investors are paying attention to corporate environmental and social records.*

As you read, consider the following questions:

1. What does it mean to say that there is "a strong business case" for purchasing a fleet of low-emission vehicles, as John Lorinc reports that Purolator is doing?
2. What explanation does the author give for why companies' voluntary disclosure reports are now being pushed to provide better quantitative analysis?
3. Lorinc mentions "an emissions credits trading system" that is maturing into "a legitimate market." What is being traded in this system?

One doesn't need to be an expert on climate change and energy markets to realize that companies with large vehicle fleets are hurtling toward a future of rising operating costs and increasingly onerous regulation. That's why, several years ago, Canadian courier giant Purolator decided to start an experiment with delivery vehicles that rely on alternative fuels: gas-electric hybrids and hydrogen fuel-cell vans. The project began as a demonstration partnership with Azure, a hybrid-vehicle maker. But after almost a decade of steadily rising fuel prices, what began as little more than a feel-good PR [public relations] initiative has morphed into something much bigger and more profitable.

Today, there is a strong business case for changing the entire 3,000-van fleet to low-emission vehicles, says Serge Viola, Purolator's national fleet and ground line haul director. As of late 2007, Purolator was operating 49 hybrids, the company is ordering 105 more this year, another 200 in 2009, and expects to replace the entire fleet within a decade. Viola says there's a reduction of 35% to 40% in fuel consumption for each hy-

brid, plus a 15% to 20% savings on maintenance. Such a shift is a blend of sound economics and environmental steward-ship. "You want to do things right," he says, "but you have to make it viable at the same time."

## It Is Possible to Be Clean and Profitable

Such moves underscore a seismic shift occurring in corporate social responsibility (CSR). For years, progressive-minded consumers have been flocking to businesses that deal in so-cially and environmentally sustainable products and services. Organic and fair-trade foods are staple items on the shelves of supermarkets, which are falling over one another to reduce their plastic bag usage. Some clothing makers are selling ap-parel made from hemp or organic cotton. And products made out of recycled materials—everything from paper towels made from 100% recycled fibre to handbags fabricated from used tires—have gained growing consumer acceptance.

Meanwhile, some conservation-minded homeowners are investing in thermal windows, high-grade insulation and energy-efficient appliances, while others are signing on with green-energy marketers such as Toronto's Bullfrog Power. "If you call it green, you have a bit of a marketing angle," says Grant Thornton assurance partner Jeremy Jagt, a Mississauga, Ont., CA whose client roster includes several clean-energy firms. Citing the example of wind farms, he notes, "You can market something like that to the public [by saying], 'You can make a contribution to the environment by investing in my company.'"

Over the past few years, however, what's become apparent is that a growing number of companies are looking more in-tensively at their operations with an eye to using CSR initia-tives to improve their environmental and social track records, as well as the bottom line.

In some cases, such changes are motivated by regulation. Mining and oil/gas exploration companies in particular are

facing intense pressure—from governments, advocacy groups and investors—to be far better environmental stewards. But increasingly, the drivers include a radical shift in the way companies are thinking about the environment in the era of climate change uncertainty. Firms such as Brookfield Properties are creating less wasteful offices—for example, setting up recycling programs or reducing wasteful lighting. There are even more profound operational changes, as is the case with Purolator.

With the scrutiny has come a push for better quantitative analysis in voluntary disclosure reports and third-party assurance of CSR data. Glossy brochures full of environmental bromides no longer cut it, while the absence of a detailed CSR report is now noted by advocacy groups and European investors.

## Claims Must Be Verifiable

Indeed, in February [2008] the Ontario Securities Commission slammed Canadian publicly traded companies for failing to provide detailed disclosure about their environmental liabilities such as chemical spills. The commission is proposing that firms include verifiable estimates about the cost of dealing with such risks as part of their financial statements, rather than merely relying on boilerplate disclosure.

For experts such as Gordon Richardson, KPMG professor of accounting at the University of Toronto's Rotman School of Management, such changes indicate that many firms are moving beyond PR-oriented CSR reporting into a new type of sustainable management. Seeking to reduce their emissions, they are making tough operational choices and adopting rigorous reporting standards. And those decisions are being rewarded in the market. "It's the good performers who are pushing this," he says. "They want a level playing field so the poor environmental performers can't make false claims."

About five years ago, Tridel president Leo Delzotto announced to his company that it would begin constructing

apartment buildings very differently than it had been doing for decades. One of North America's largest condo builders, Tridel recognized the need to make its apartments more energy efficient as a means of dealing with rising energy costs. Over the next three or four years, Tridel manager of research and development Rambod Nasrin led a push to come up with new designs and technologies that could be marshaled to make greener buildings. He scoured the market for new lighting, insulation and heating technologies. His group proposed new layouts for the apartments and motion sensors that would turn off garage lights when no one was present.

Today, Tridel is building a dozen projects that will qualify for the Leadership in Energy and Environmental Design (LEED) standard for green design. In each, energy efficiency has been increased by 25% to 35%, which translates into reduced emissions as well as savings worth as much as $100,000 to $200,000 a year for an average high-rise condominium. Environmental design, Nasrin says, "is becoming the market standard. In the next five years, you'll be hard pressed to find buildings not designed this way."

Nasrin freely admits that consumers, while interested, aren't exactly lining up for energy-efficient condos. Rather, Tridel's shift is a case of a company retooling its business practices to confront the looming risks linked to energy and climate change.

For large firms, such changes also represent a means of demonstrating to investors, consumers, advocacy groups and regulators that they're doing more good than harm. Pointing to the performance of the Dow Jones Sustainability Indexes, CSR experts also say that such efforts do bolster the bottom line and boost share price.

## CSR Pays Off

CSR has "really taken off in the past 24 months," says Peter Johnson, PricewaterhouseCoopers' director of sustainable busi-

"Professor Linetti will now illustrate how to put social responsibility ahead of profits in order to make even more profits." Cartoon by Piero Tonin. www.CartoonStock. com.

ness solutions in Toronto. There's been a rapid run-up in the number of publicly traded firms issuing sustainability reports designed to position these companies as good corporate citizens. A growing number conform to international CSR disclosure standards, such as the Global Reporting Initiative. "CSR is a lens for how a company is managed," adds Johnson. "If a firm is managing its social and environmental responsibilities in an open way, it's assumed to be better managed than one just focused on commercial objectives."

Those assumptions, as often as not, are made by shareholders pressing for operational changes and better data. This

year, for example, 315 global investors representing $41 trillion in assets signed on to The Carbon Disclosure Project, requesting disclosure from companies around the world, including the top 200 TSX [Toronto Stock Exchange] firms. "Investors want to know if companies have considered the [business] risks associated with climate change," says Valerie Chort, a partner and national leader of Deloitte's corporate responsibility and sustainability services in Toronto. "That's driving a lot of disclosure."

Chort also predicts that the availability of such data will only grow as the carbon economy, in the form of an emission credits trading system, matures into a genuine market. She says a number of financial institutions are developing funds to hold and trade carbon assets, and such instruments have begun to have a market value.

## Hidden Liabilities Can Do Harm

Richardson adds that latent environmental liabilities, particularly those linked to emissions and inefficient energy use, clearly have the potential to morph into onerous future expenses. "If standards are ratcheted up, these companies will be forced to spend."

The rub is that environmental accounting is still very much an emerging field. "Accounting for sustainability costs is very difficult," admits Christine Schuh, Canadian climate change services leader for PricewaterhouseCoopers in Calgary. "It's a gray area." With greenhouse gases, for example, firms are still trying to figure out how to allocate funds that are being used to invest in emission reduction technology. "When you reduce greenhouse gases, you're increasing the efficiency of the plant," says Schuh. "Is that considered an improvement or a compliance requirement?"

Lawyer Melanie Steiner, a senior manager with Ernst & Young's risk advisory services in Toronto, notes that in a growing number of companies, the impetus for change begins at

the board, which establishes a sustainability or environment committee to develop broad principles that are turned over to the CEO for implementation. Such governance initiatives, she adds, are linked to the risk-management ethos of the Sarbanes-Oxley era. But, Steiner notes, "innovative companies are looking at this in a more strategic way."

Once corporate leaders have signaled their intentions, as happened with Tridel, buy in from senior management becomes a crucial next step. "A new generation of CEOs is more interested in these broader issues. They take the board mandate and filter it down to all levels of the organization," says Steiner.

Depending on the firm, those CSR directives may be focused on reducing workplace accidents, increasing community engagement or making operations more environmentally sustainable. Johnson, for instance, says some major retailers are pressing such policies down the supply chain, asking for assurances about labour standards or demanding less packaging. "Any company that has a brand or reputation that is front and centre in the public eye—those are the ones pushing ahead with this."

Not surprisingly, Steiner points out, companies are adding lawyers, engineers, MBAs and other technical experts to their internal audit departments as they gear up to measure and confirm CSR initiatives. Some firms also retain outside consultants to audit their own operations or those of their suppliers.

## Benefits Emerge over Time

Robert Kolida, senior vice-president of human resources at Hudson's Bay Co. [HBC], says such changes don't happen overnight. HBC issued its first CSR report in 2001–2002 and estimates it has found about $9 million in efficiency-related savings since then. Initially, the retailer's sustainability program looked at low-hanging fruit, such as installing energy-efficient lighting and printing documents on double-sided pa-

per. As the company begins to realize savings, its CSR initiatives—branded internally as Global Mind—continue to expand. Like many retailers, HBC is now working to reduce packaging by promoting reusable bags. Its trucks use cleaner bio-diesel fuel and HBC has opened a new Zellers store, in Waterdown, Ont., that has roof-top wind turbines.

The company, moreover, has set up internal reporting systems to encourage employees to bring forward other ideas to Kolida's group, which spearheads HBC's sustainability efforts. "It's not something we'll do this year and then we're done," he says. "Our managers have bought in to the Global Mind philosophy. That's when CSR programs take off."

Much of the attention, of course, is directed toward the natural resources sectors—forestry, pulp and paper, mining, and oil and gas exploration. Companies operating in these sectors, as Schuh says, "don't want to see a big spill or a large operational failure that results in deaths." The Exxon Valdez oil spill in 1989 was not just an environmental disaster; it swiftly decimated the goodwill and reputation of one of the world's largest companies.

The resource extraction industry has come under heavy scrutiny for all the obvious reasons: unflattering accounts of corruption, dismal working conditions and environmental degradation linked to the conduct of Canadian mining and oil/gas exploration firms doing business in developing nations. In March 2007 the National Roundtables on Corporate Social Responsibility and the Canadian Extractive Industry in Developing Countries . . . issued a report recommending that companies pay far more attention to meeting CSR standards for mine closures, community engagement and fair wages or face losing federal export assistance.

## Finding Common Ground Can Be Difficult

Industry groups, in sectors such as pulp and paper, mining and forestry, are now trying to find ways of urging their members to adopt the recommendations and implement sectoral

sustainability reporting standards, says Richardson. "It's contentious because for some members, it's not in their best interests to develop these standards."

But Vince Borg, Barrick Gold's senior vice-president of corporate communications, says meaningful CSR has to be "part of a company's DNA," not just an exercise in damage control or PR. He recalls that one of Barrick's earliest CSR moves, back when the firm had only a few Quebec mines, was to offer university scholarships to the children of its employees as a means of encouraging them to stick with the company. The perk was about enlightened self-interest: the company had trained its employees and wanted to protect its investment. "It proved to be an effective means of retaining our skilled employees."

Nearly two decades later, Borg says, Barrick has continued to take this approach with its mining operations in Latin America. The company goes out of its way to invest millions in the physical and social infrastructure of the communities where its mines are located—roads, schools, etc. That strategy has paid off in Peru, where there's been growing labour unrest in recent years. Barrick, says Borg, hasn't experienced any major disruptions and its mines remained open during a nationwide wildcat strike last fall.

Indeed, when Barrick officials recently held their quarterly conference call, investment analysts were curious about how the firm dodged the labour disruption bullet when so many other mining firms had experienced work stoppages. Borg points out that the company has never had to downgrade its annual guidance to investors—a prediction about production volumes—due to strikes. His point: being socially responsible is smart management, and investors will reward them for it.

"It's totally quantifiable," he says. "The goodwill [created] has affected the value of this asset."

Of course, the financial benefits aren't just apparent to investors, as Tom Farley, president and chief operating officer of

Brookfield Properties, explains. Over the past five years, the real estate giant has systematically invested in improved heating, lighting, ventilation, water and waste-management systems in its office buildings. The firm installs hydro meters in its tenants' premises and encourages them to cut their energy consumption. It installed low-flush toilets in one new development and is putting them into some older buildings as well. And in Toronto's Brookfield Place an internal recycling program has increased diversion rates to an impressive 89%.

The financial benefits are now coming home to roost. Last year, the company realized a 15% reduction in hydro bills thanks to the installation of new chillers in one of its buildings—a $600,000 savings for its tenants. New lighting sensors: a $400,000 savings. Digitally controlled temperature and airflow systems: $450,000 a year. By reducing its tenants' costs, the company is better positioned to retain them.

"The bottom line," says Farley, "is that going green creates both environmental and financial incentives for the building owner and the tenants."

"*Many organizations are today espousing a 'green' strategy. . . . It must be a genuine and challenging 'quest' for progress, characterized by a change in leadership behaviour . . . if it is to succeed rather than be castigated as 'greenwashing' or a public relations 'scam.'*"

# A Credible Green Strategy Begins with Real Personal and Organizational Change

*Tim Osborn-Jones*

*Tim Osborn-Jones, a member of the faculty at the School of Leadership, Change and HR Management at Henley Management College, makes the case in this viewpoint that corporate social responsibility needs to be grounded in real personal and behavioral change on the part of organizational leaders. He maintains that behaviors drive outcomes, and behavioral change must result from reflection on experience and constructive critical thinking, in a collaborative process that has the power to change both individuals and organizations.*

Tim Osborn-Jones, "How to Find a Sustainable Process," *Training Journal*, December 2007, pp. 47–50. © 2007 Training Journal. Reproduced by permission.

As you read, consider the following questions:

1. What role do climate change and global warming play in the decision of some corporations to operate in a more sustainable way?

2. What role does collaboration play in bringing about the kind of behavioral change in which the author is interested?

3. The author talks about "communities of practice" that are necessary for transformative learning to take place. What are the characteristics of a community of practice?

Responding to the challenge of sustainable development is critical for long-term competitive advantage. It will drive greater efficiencies, innovation, and positive reputation. As the *Stern Review*, and other climate change reports make clear, the economic costs and social disruption of global warming are going to be on an unprecedented scale if we do not make a concerned effort to bring in more sustainable ways of producing wealth and social well-being in the near future.

Sustainability is also viewed in terms of corporate governance, reputation and responsibility, often summarised as corporate social responsibility (CSR). Aspects of responsibility are drivers of reputation, and reputation in stakeholder relationships is a key driver of business success. [K.] Money & [C.] Hillenbrand identify three high-level themes to represent the ways in which customers and employees understand corporate responsibility:

1. *"The way a business relates to me as a customer or employee"*—essentially how they are treated in terms of core business activities.

2. *"The way a business relates to others"*—essentially how a business relates to other stakeholder groups such as the employees, customers, suppliers or the local community.

3. *"The way a business relates to itself"*—essentially a business's long-term profitability and viability.

In the minds of stakeholders, a business is responsible for how it relates to 'me', 'others' and 'itself'. Similarly, 'my' behaviours have an impact on, and drive an outcome for, 'me' as an individual, 'others' (e.g. my community) and 'my' organisation. Individuals and organizations face multiple stakeholders: we are all in this together, and increasingly relationships are judged in terms of values, such as 'integrity, transparency and accountability', and how it 'makes one feel'.

## Behaviours Drive Outcomes

These aspects of reputation are captured in the Henley 'Competency Star' model of managerial effectiveness. Competencies come in various 'flavours', sometimes known as 'input', 'process' and 'outcome' competencies. Managers and leaders need a range of 'inputs', knowledge and understanding, awareness of their personal characteristics, and skills to inform and facilitate their effective behaviours ('process competencies'), which, in turn, lead to 'outcomes'. These are combined as the basis of an approach to personal and leadership development.

## Beyond Science to a Process

Many organisations are today espousing a green strategy. [As described by S.J. Downing,] it must be a genuine and challenging 'quest' for progress, characterised by a change in leadership behaviours and leading to a change in organisational behaviour, if it is to succeed rather than be castigated as 'greenwashing' or a public relations 'scam'. The challenge of sustainability is to establish approaches to personal and leadership development that will engender change in individual and organisational behaviour; a process that will help managers and leaders:

- reflect on, and identify, their values,

- listen to their stakeholders and identify any difference in values,

- deal with dilemmas arising.

In response to these demands, managers need to reflect on, and explore, their own values and beliefs as a basis for action. Learning processes need to be reviewed. The focus is on collaborative, constructive, and critical active learning to help managers manage dilemmas, make choices and live with the consequences:

- *Collaboration.* Managers learn most effectively when they work together with a shared purpose, facilitated by faculty (both subject matter and process tutors). There are three key components of collaboration:

- *Personal development.* Self-awareness leads to individual and team development.

- *Reflection and feedback.* Managers learn through reflecting on their values, experiences and needs in a different environment, and by putting new learning and ideas into practice, related to their needs, with the help of faculty and peers.

- *Communication.* Participants need to be committed and open to new learning and change, to share their knowledge, skills, and experiences.

- *Constructive critical thinking.* The learning process involves challenging knowledge, skills and behaviours but not driving competition among learners. In order for learning to be both effective and to become embedded, managers need to question themselves and others; through this they will develop new insights and new ideas.

In summary, teaching and learning with mid-career executives should be underpinned by three core values:

1. the power of facilitated group learning;

---

**The Henley Competency Star**

*A Model of Managerial Effectiveness*

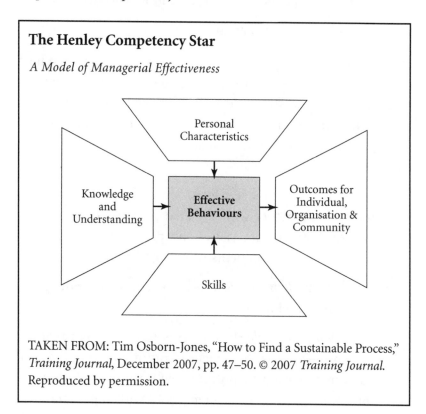

TAKEN FROM: Tim Osborn-Jones, "How to Find a Sustainable Process," *Training Journal*, December 2007, pp. 47–50. © 2007 *Training Journal*. Reproduced by permission.

---

2. the enhancing quality of personal development; and

3. the real-world authority of action.

## New Learning Approaches to Sustainability

Building on these principles of experiential learning, new learning approaches need to be explored, particularly in order to reflect the global and cross-cultural dimensions of working for sustainability. Examples of these are:

- *Communities of practice.* Communities of practice take much from the notion of 'situated learning', that learning is a function of the activity, context and culture in which it occurs. This contrasts with most classroom learning activities, which involve knowledge that is abstract and out of context. Social interaction is a critical

component of situated learning—learners become involved in a community of practice that embodies certain beliefs and behaviours to be acquired, such as bonding by exposure to common problems, common practices and language, and a common sense of purpose.

Groups that learn—communities of practice—have special characteristics. They emerge of their own accord; three, four, 20, maybe 30 people find themselves drawn to one another by a force that's both social and professional. They collaborate directly, use one another as sounding boards, and teach each other.

Communities of practice are everywhere. We all belong to a number of them—at work, at school, at home, in our hobbies. Some have a name, some don't. We are core members of some and we belong to others more peripherally. You may be a member of a band, or you may just come to rehearsals to hang around with the group. You may lead a group of consultants who specialise in telecommunication strategies, or you may just stay in touch to keep informed about developments in the field. Or you may have just joined a community and are still trying to find your place in it.

Whatever forms our participation take, most of us are familiar with the experience of belonging to a community of practice.

Communities of practice also exist in many organisations. Membership is based on participation rather than official status; communities are not bound by organisational affiliations. They span institutional structures and hierarchies.

*Action enquiry and collaborative research.* Closely related to the notion of community of practice, action enquiry describes research undertaken on a collaborative basis between academic and practitioner: expert process guidance is supplied to support rigorous enquiry on a topic of interest and importance to the practitioner, leading to evidence-based, improved practice. Research into the impact of collaborative research

91

and action enquiry at Henley suggests that this approach has the greatest power to enable organisations to challenge their own dominant logic and question their place in the world in ways that draw strength, insight and inspiration from each other.

*Immersion.* "Tell me and I will forget; show me and I may remember; involve me and I will understand" (Confucius 450 BC). Precisely because it is behaviours that drive outcomes; it is important to change behaviours, to direct them to the intended outcome. This is especially true of those behaviours that reflect deep and often subconsciously held values. Immersion in unfamiliar social, cultural and business environments can offer transformational experiences and prompt an emotional trigger, leading by way of reflection to new ways of knowing, through intellect, memory, senses, intuition or imagination.

*Mindfulness.* The transition to sustainable development requires radical innovation of production and consumption, energy use and business models. P. Senge *et al* have found that profoundly innovative individuals have to become aware of their own perceptual lenses, and let go of conventional ways of seeing, before innovative ways of seeing and doing can emerge. Their Theory U describes a process of sensing (transforming perception), presencing (transforming self and will) and realising (acting with the flow). [S.J.] Downing sets out a process using the SENSE tool to help individuals become aware of the organisational stories that shape perception and the inner dialogue that builds or undermines leadership capability.

These approaches reflect what [Richard E.] Boyatsis *et al* have called 'mindfulness'. This is a state of being that is fully aware of self, others and the environment; a process that enables a leader to connect others to big ideas like sustainability while maintaining hope and compassion: a quest for sustainability.

"*The use of the term 'greenwashing' is enjoying a resurgence and has entered the mainstream. A search of the Nexis news archive turned up more than 700 mentions of the term in the [first six months of 2008] alone.*"

# Some Companies Are Not Honest About Their Environmental Records

*Phil Mattera*

*In this viewpoint Phil Mattera, research director of Good Jobs First, argues that the current wave of corporate environmentalism is rooted in deception more than in fact, and that the public is becoming more skeptical in interpreting these claims. He points to* The Wall Street Journal *and* Business Week, *who have each published articles challenging the claims of companies that are engaging in green marketing campaigns. Mattera states that marketing firms are coming clean about "the sins of greenwashing" and government regulators and private watchdog groups are looking more closely, and more critically, at companies who claim to have adopted environmentally friendly business practices.*

Phil Mattera, "Is Corporate Greenwashing Headed for a Fall?" *Alternet*, February 12, 2008. Reproduced by permission of the author.

93

As you read, consider the following questions:

1. The author of this viewpoint compares the current green marketing efforts of corporations with the dot com boom that eventually deflated, and with the real estate credit crunch. What point is he trying to make with these comparisons?

2. How does the author view the environmental policies of the President George W. Bush administration?

3. TerraChoice, a marketing firm, published a paper about greenwashing recently which discussed "the sin of the hidden trade-off." To what does that phrase refer?

Imagine you are a communication technician on a planet in another solar system that is facing an ecological disaster and is looking for new solutions. One day you suddenly pick up broadcast signals from Earth that happen to include a man talking to a group of children sitting beside a hulking vehicle he is describing as a "vegetarian" because it uses a fuel called ethanol. The segment ends with the statement: "Chevy: from gas-friendly to gas-free. That's an American revolution."

Then you get a transmission from something called BP, [a multinational oil company] that is talking about going beyond—beyond darkness, beyond fear, beyond petroleum. Another from Toyota shows a vehicle being put together like a grass hut and then disintegrating back into nature without a trace. The messages keep coming—from General Electric [GE] ("eco-imagination"), Chevron (celebrating the miraculous power of "human energy") and so on.

As you receive more of these signals, you rush to your superiors and announce the good news: Planet Earth has wonderful entities called corporations that can solve all our environmental problems.

Residents of our planet may be tempted to jump to the same conclusion. These days we are bombarded with advertisements that want us to believe that major oil companies,

automakers and other large corporations are solving the environmental and energy problems facing the earth. Fear not global warming, peak oil, polluted air and water—big business will take care of everything.

In the late 1990s we saw a hyped-up dot com boom that came crashing down. In the past year or so, we have seen a hyped real estate boom turn into a credit crunch and an unprecedented number of home foreclosures. Are we now seeing a green business boom that will also turn out to be nothing more than hot air?

## The "Green Con"

Today's surge of corporate environmentalism is not the first time business has sought to align itself with public concerns about the fate of the earth. Two decades ago, marketers began to recognize the benefits of appealing to green consumers. This revelation first took hold in countries such as Britain and Canada. For example, in early 1989 the giant British supermarket chain Tesco launched a campaign to promote the products on its shelves that were deemed "environmentally friendly." That same year, Canadian mining giant Inco Ltd. began running ads promoting its effort to reduce sulfur emissions from its smelters, conveniently failing to mention it was doing so under government orders.

In 1990 the green business wave spread to the United States in time to coincide with the 20th annual Earth Day [April 22] celebration. Large U.S. companies such as DuPont [chemical company] began touting their environmental initiatives and staged their own Earth Tech environmental technology fair on the National Mall [in Washington, DC]. General Motors ran ads emphasizing its supposed concern about the environment, despite its continuing resistance to significant increases in fuel efficiency requirements.

Such exercises in corporate image-burnishing did not have a great deal of impact. For one thing, environmental groups

wasted no time debunking the ads. In 1989 Friends of the Earth in Britain gave "Green Con" awards to those companies that made the most exaggerated and unsubstantiated environmental claims about their products. First prize went to British National Fuels for promoting nuclear power as friendly to the environment.

Greenpeace USA staged a protest at the 1990 corporate Earth Tech fair, denouncing companies such as DuPont for trying to whitewash their poor environmental record with green claims. Greenpeace's invented term for this practice—greenwashing—immediately caught on, and to this day is a succinct way of undermining dubious corporate claims about the environment.

The general public was also not taken in by the corporate environmental push of 1989–1990. It was just a bit too obvious that these initiatives were meant to deflect attention away from recent environmental disasters such as the Exxon Valdez oil spill in Alaska and Union Carbide's deadly Bhopal chemical leak. It also didn't help that many of the claims about green products turned out to be misleading or meaningless.

## "Green Lies"

The question today is whether people have become more receptive to corporate environmental hype. One thing business has going for it in the United States is that the [George W.] Bush administration has pursued environmental policies so retrograde that even the most superficial green measures by the private sector shine in comparison. Another is that some environmental groups have switched from an outside adversarial strategy to a more collaborative approach that often involves forming partnerships with companies. Such relationships serve to legitimize business initiatives while turning those groups into cheerleaders for their corporate partners. Former Sierra Club president Adam Werbach took it a step further and joined the payroll of Wal-Mart.

Illustration by Tom Fishburne. Illustration courtesy of Tom Fishburne.

On the other hand, the use of the term "greenwashing" is enjoying a resurgence and has entered the mainstream. A search of the Nexis news archive turned up more than 700 mentions of the term in the [first six months of 2008] alone. Even that bible of the marketing world—*Advertising Age*—recently published a list titled "The Green and the Greenwashed: Ten Who Get It and 10 Who Talk a Good Game." Among the latter were General Motors, Toyota, ExxonMobil, Chevron, Wal-Mart, General Electric and Ikea, though Toyota, Wal-Mart and Ikea were also put on the green list for other reasons.

Other business publications have also been taking a more critical approach to green claims. [In September of 2007,] *The Wall Street Journal* looked behind GE's eco-imagination campaign and found all was not well. For one thing, there was significant resistance even within GE's managerial ranks and among many of the conglomerate's major industrial custom-

ers. Then there was the fact that GE was still pushing big-
ticket products such as coal-fired steam turbines that were significant contributors to global warming. Finally, the paper
pointed out that the campaign was motivated in substantial
part by a desire to increase sales of existing GE products such
as wind turbines that could be promoted as eco-friendly.

In October [2007], *Business Week* published a cover story
titled "Little Green Lies." It began with the declaration: "The
sweet notion that making a company environmentally friendly
can be not just cost-effective but profitable is going up in
smoke." The piece featured Auden Schendler of Aspen Skiing
Company, a pioneer in adopting environmentally friendly
practices. After showing off his company's energy-efficient facilities, he was described as having turned to the *Business
Week* reporter and said: "Who are we kidding?" He then acknowledged that the growth of the company necessarily means
burning more power, including the ever-increasing energy
needed to create artificial snow during warmer winters. "How
do you really green your company? It's almost f------ impossible."

## The Six Sins

Another factor working against corporate hype is that critics
are becoming more systematic in their critique of greenwashing. In November [2007], a marketing firm called TerraChoice
did an analysis of more than 1,000 products bearing environmental claims. After finding that all but one of those claims
were false or misleading in some respect, TerraChoice issued a
paper called *The Six Sins of Greenwashing* that analyzed the
various forms of deception.

The most common shortcoming found by TerraChoice is
the "sin of the hidden trade-off," in which a single positive at-
tribute of a product is promoted while ignoring the detrimental environmental impact of the whole manufacturing process.
For example, paper that has some recycled content but is pro-

duced in a way that causes serious air and water pollution as well as entailing a large amount of greenhouse gas emissions. The other sins listed by TerraChoice are no proof, vagueness, irrelevance, lesser of two evils and fibbing.

Do-it-yourself greenwashing criticism is now possible through a Web site recently launched by EnviroMedia Social Marketing. Its Greenwashing Index site allows users to post ads—usually video footage taken from YouTube—and rate them on a scale of 1 (good ad) to 5 (total greenwashing).

More troubling, from the corporate perspective, are signs that government regulators and industry-established watchdog groups are giving more scrutiny to green claims. Last month [May 2008], the UK's [United Kingdom's] Advertising Standards Authority found that a series of television ads being run around the world by the Malaysian Palm Oil Council contained misleading statements about the environmental benefits of its product. Several months ago, government regulators in Norway banned automobile ads from stating that any cars are environmentally friendly, given their contribution to global warming.

Even in the United States there are signs that regulators may be getting concerned about greenwashing. The Federal Trade Commission, which in 1992 issued national guidelines for environmental marketing claims but has done little on the subject since then, announced in November [2007] that it was beginning a review of its guidelines.

## Unclean Hands and Excessive Size

Corporations, no doubt, will not give up their environmental claims without a fight. Perhaps the hardest nut to crack will be Wal-Mart. For the past couple of years, the giant retailer has depicted itself as being on a crusade to address global warming and other environmental issues—a crusade it wants its suppliers, its workers and its customers to join. In October 2005, CEO Lee Scott gave a speech in which he embraced

sweeping goals to reduce greenhouse gas emissions and raise energy efficiency. Last month he gave another speech that re-affirmed those goals and upped the ante by envisioning a future in which Wal-Mart customers would drive to the store in electric cars that could be recharged in the parking lot using power generated by wind turbines and solar panels.

Wal-Mart's greenwashing involves sins beyond those listed by TerraChoice. First, there is the sin of unclean hands. It is difficult to avoid thinking that the company is using its environmental initiatives to draw attention away from its widely criticized labor practices—both in its own stores and in the factories of its low-wage suppliers abroad. Until the company provides decent working conditions, respects the right of its employees to unionize and ceases to sell goods made by sweat-shop labor, Wal-Mart cannot expect to be a paradigm of social responsibility.

Then there's the sin of size. A company as large as Wal-Mart will inevitably have a negative effect on the countries from which it obtains its goods, the agricultural areas from which it gets it food products, and the communities where it locates its big-box stores. There's a growing sense that true sustainability entails a substantial degree of localism and moderate-size enterprise. That rules out Wal-Mart, no matter what its CEO professes.

Wal-Mart's problem may be the problem of big business as a whole. As hard as they try to convince us, huge profit-maximizing transnational corporations may never be true friends of the environment. Let's hope this message also gets through to those listening in distant worlds.

> *"Just as ad agencies are being challenged to respond to climate change mania, so are communication practitioners. In fact, you could argue that never before has so much been at stake for the corporate communication industry."*

# Climate Change Is a Problem Corporate Communications Professionals Must Address

### Chris Freimond

*Chris Freimond, a corporate communications consultant in Vancouver, British Columbia, argues in this viewpoint that widespread concern about climate change is a fact of life for communications professionals. No organization is shielded from scrutiny about its environmental practices, and no organization is immune from criticism, he says. Freimond maintains that communications professionals need to understand the issue and communicate with their organization's leadership to develop and implement a climate change communications program that addresses in an honest way the organization's environmental impacts.*

Chris Freimond, "Global Warming Reaches the Boardroom," *Communication World*, November-December 2007, pp. 22–24. © 2007 International Association of Business Communicators. Reproduced by permission.

As you read, consider the following questions:

1. The author uses the example of a small law firm as an organization that might mistakenly think that its operations do not have an environmental impact. Why does he suggest that this assumption is not correct?

2. The marketing community has become increasingly interested in climate change. Why is this important, according to the author?

3. What does the author say is the first step to take in addressing climate change in a business setting?

G iven the global preoccupation with climate change, it's no surprise that corporate marketers have moved quickly to place "green" products front and center. Automobile companies boast climate-friendly, best-in-class gas mileage, and oil companies spend more on telling consumers what they're doing to protect the environment than they do on selling their products.

But just as ad agencies are being challenged to respond to climate change mania, so are communication practitioners. In fact, you could argue that never before has so much been at stake for the corporate communication industry.

## The Climate Change Phenomenon

While corporate social responsibility (CSR) in its many incarnations evolved relatively slowly—allowing communicators to come to terms with how it affected their work—climate change has become a sociopolitical phenomenon with PR [public relations] implications that are still relatively new and largely unknown.

What does this mean for communicators? Some organizations believe that they don't contribute to climate change and therefore have nothing to communicate. That is a mistake. A small law firm, for example, could argue that its operations have no direct impact on global pollution. But the reams of

paper it uses do, and the automobiles driven by partners and staff do, and the air conditioning that cools their offices, and the lights they leave on at night—the list goes on.

This type of scrutiny goes way beyond what we've traditionally regarded as CSR. Now we're talking about personal behavior and habits. For smaller organizations that are not overt polluters, these are the types of issues that need to be considered when responding to climate change. They will increasingly become measures of good corporate citizenship and could play a significant role in consumer choice.

Equally important is knowing how to respond when critics come calling. It's not inconceivable that environmental activist groups, emboldened by the mainstreaming of green issues, will start asking questions about the business operations of more than just the usual suspects.

## Audiences Are More Aware of the Issues

Solitaire Townsend, managing director of London-based Futerra Sustainability Communications, believes communicating about responsible business practices is more of a challenge as audiences become increasingly aware of ethical issues. In a 6 February [2006] article for ClimateChangeCorp.com, a web site of climate change news for the business community, she said that growing interest in climate change by the marketing community is evidence that CSR has become mainstream.

"It is a relief," she writes, "to find a whole page dedicated to avoiding greenwash. Indeed the Advertising Standards Authority has begun to flex its muscles on green claims and CSR, noting that sweeping statements such as environmentally friendly' or 'zero environmental legacy' will be challenged."

Communicators who work for companies that already have good CSR programs in place probably don't need to do much; those whose companies don't have cogent CSR policies should seriously consider doing something about it. But that doesn't mean rushing head-long into an ill-conceived program

## Adapting to Climate Change

The firms that will prosper in a climate-changed world will tend to be those that are: early to recognise its importance and its inexorability; foresee at least some of the implications for their industry; and take appropriate steps well in advance.

This is likely to involve, within an overall framework of good management practice:

- Inculcating in management a constructive culture of adaptation to a changing economic landscape;

- Encouraging employees to embrace change, and equipping them to do so;

- Undertaking the requisite research and development, which is often highly industry- or even firm-specific; and

- Translating this research and development into appropriate investment in physical and human capital.

The pace of a firm's adaptation to climate change and related policy is thus likely to prove to be another of the forces that will influence whether, over the next several years, any given firm survives and prospers; or withers and, quite possibly, dies.

*John Llewellyn, "The Business of Climate Change:*
*Challenges and Opportunities," February 2007.*
*http://lehmantrust.b.z.*

that neither addresses the real issues of climate change nor serves the best interests of the organization. The following steps are a guide to getting on top of climate change in a business setting.

*Research and understand the issue.* Make sure you know what climate change is and what it's doing to the planet. Find out what regulators are doing and saying that could affect your organization. Do your own research on how your organization and your business sector affect climate change. If you have the resources for further research, do independent polling to see what stakeholders think of your performance.

*Present your findings to your organization's leadership.* Look carefully at what's possible and what's not—strategically and operationally—and consider how you would communicate actions (or inaction) to stakeholders. Get leadership buy-in and a commitment to actively support the program.

*Develop a plan (or update your existing CSR plan).* Align your climate change communication program with your organization's strategic plan. Don't neglect employees in the planning process. They need as much help as anyone else in sorting through the information overload.

*Implement the plan sensibly and sensitively.* Remember, in many respects this is just another component of CSR, but it needs to address your specific organization's impact on climate change. Use your organization's influence to raise stakeholder awareness of the dangers of climate change and encourage actions to reduce its impact.

# Periodical Bibliography

*The following articles have been selected to supplement the diverse views presented in this chapter.*

Christian Bellavance     "Going Green: Corporate Social Responsibility Has Evolved from a Feel-Good Initiative to a Bottom Line Contributor," *CA Magazine*, May 2008.

Temma Ehrenfeld     "Green, or Greenwash?" *Newsweek*, July 14, 2008.

Daniel Fisher     "Selling the Blue Sky," *Forbes*, February 25, 2008.

Bill McKibben     "Hype vs. Hope: Is Corporate Do-Goodery for Real?" *Mother Jones*, November–December 2006.

Elizabeth Palmberg     "Do the Math: Don't Buy the Corporate Agro-fuel Greenwash," *Sojourners Magazine*, January 2008.

Alex Palmer     "Corporate Social Responsibility: Patagonia Reconnects with Its Roots," *Incentive*, July 7, 2008.

C.J. Prince     "It's Not Easy Being Green: It's Tough to Separate the Hype from Reality When It Comes to Environmentally Friendly Initiatives. But Those Companies That Do Stand to Gain Big," *Chief Executive*, January–February 2008.

N. Ravindran     "Community Outreach Through Corporate Social Responsibility," *Today's Manager*, December–January 2008.

Jess Worth     "Companies Who Care? Jess Worth Ventures into the World of Corporate Responsibility and Finds It Not Just Dumb but Dangerous," *New Internationalist*, December 2007.

OPPOSING
VIEWPOINTS®
SERIES

CHAPTER 3

# Do Corporations Have a Social Responsibility to Protect Human Rights?

# Chapter Preface

The claim that a product is manufactured in such a way that no harm is done to human beings, animals or the environment is a key element of many corporate social responsibility (CSR) initiatives. Manufacturing practices that are viewed as socially responsible may incur additional expense, and because this expense is undertaken voluntarily, it doesn't necessarily make sense from a purely financial point of view. On paper, voluntary CSR measures can make an enterprise seem less profitable. However, CSR is typically seen as a marketing strategy that works by appealing to the sensibilities of "ethical consumers"—individuals for whom value is added when a product is manufactured in a socially responsible way. Such individuals, it is argued, are willing to pay premium prices for goods that are produced according to a higher ethical standard.

As an example, in the spring of 2008 a Canadian jewelry retailer announced it had entered into an exclusive agreement to distribute Botswana Diamonds, a brand, at its stores in Canada and the United States. "These diamonds are exclusively sourced through DTC Botswana and manufactured at [Diamond Manufacturing Botswana's] state-of-the-art factory," the Birks & Mayors' press release noted. A senior vice president for Birks & Mayors, who identified the company as an industry leader in the support of socially responsible diamond sourcing, praised the partnership because it would "allow . . . us to further strengthen the chain of custody from [diamond] mine to the [showroom] case while increasing the prosperity of Botswana people." This is an important distinction. In war-torn African countries, blood diamonds, or conflict diamonds, are often mined to raise money for armaments. The United Nations defines conflict diamonds as diamonds that originate "from areas controlled by forces or

factions opposed to legitimate and internationally recognized governments." It is sometimes claimed that rebel governments that traffic in diamonds employ slave labor and commit other human rights abuses.

The Birks & Mayors' press release did not detail the specific circumstances that assured the ethical quality of the company's supply chain. But it did note that the country of Botswana depends almost exclusively on the diamond industry to provide employment, housing, health care and schools for its people. This was an appeal to ethical consumers, because buying a Botswana diamond was portrayed as a way of supporting a just lifestyle for the people of Botswana.

However, an article in *Maclean's* magazine that appeared shortly after the Botswana partnership was announced raised questions about these claims:

> "The ... jeweler is ... suggesting that when you buy one of its new Botswana diamonds, not only will your money be kept away from Africa's violent conflicts, but it will actually help to make the world a better place.... But can you be sure the rock you're buying is really from Botswana? ...
>
> Even if the glitter you get is from Botswana, it's hard to tell how much your purchase is helping the country's citizens ...
>
> Given the starting price of $3500 ... [one] question is how much consumers are willing to pay for that peace of mind."

In the new global economy, distrust is common and sensitivity about fair labor practices and human rights abuses runs high. News travels fast. The *Maclean's* article was titled "Your Bling Can Save the World." The questions posed in it illustrate how companies that market their products to ethical consumers must find ways to support their claims in order to establish credibility.

Do corporations have a social responsibility to protect human rights, and to improve the lives of the people who work

for them? Or is this an unnecessary expense? Is there really a market for socially responsible products such as conflict free diamonds? And if there is, how do firms build the kind of credibility and trust consumers require if they are to pay the "social responsibility premium?" Perhaps most important, are market forces alone enough to ensure that human rights violations do not occur, or are stronger measures needed? These are some of the issues that are explored in this chapter.

> "It is safe to say that much has changed over the past decade, and there is much to celebrate in this 60th year of the Universal Declaration of Human Rights. But it is also clear that a great deal of work remains."

# Corporations Have a Social Responsibility to Protect Human Rights

*Mary Robinson*

*Mary Robinson was the first woman president of Ireland from 1990 to 1997. She also served as the United Nations High Commissioner for Human Rights from 1997 to 2002. In this article, written to mark the sixtieth anniversary of the United Nations Declaration of Human Rights, Robinson asserts that, though much progress has been made, human rights continue to be threatened around the world. Business managers need guidance on how to integrate human rights protections into their daily operations, and more attention needs to be focused on the primary responsibility of governments to protect human rights, she says. Robinson argues that structures need to be developed to ensure*

Mary Robinson, "Human Rights: Everybody's Business," *Compact Quarterly*, April 28, 2008. Reproduced by permission.

*that private and state-owned enterprises in emerging markets are accountable for their human rights practices.*

As you read, consider the following questions:

1. What was the occasion that led Mary Robinson to write this viewpoint on human rights?
2. What are some of the reasons Mary Robinson lists that corporate leaders are taking human rights concerns seriously?
3. Who are "The Elders" named by Robinson, and what are they committed to accomplishing?

The campaign to mark the 60th anniversary of the Universal Declaration of Human Rights (UDHR) during 2008 is well underway. At a time when human rights continue to be under threat around the world, the anniversary is an important reminder that the Universal Declaration belongs to all of us, and is our shared responsibility.

But what does the 60th anniversary mean for business? Where do we stand on the often controversial subject of business and human rights?

## Acknowledging Accomplishments

First, we should acknowledge the progress made by many corporate leaders over the past decade in understanding the relevance of human rights. In 1998, the Global Compact and other efforts to link human rights to the corporate social responsibility agenda had not yet come into being. Ten years later, the "business case" is accepted by many corporate leaders who recognize that managing legal and operational risk and reputation, meeting shareholder and stakeholder expectations, and maintaining and motivating staff performance are all good reasons for taking human rights concerns seriously.

Second, today few question the central tenet that "all organs of society" (as the Universal Declaration puts it), includ-

## Why Human Rights Are Important for Business

The responsibility for human rights does not rest with governments or nation states alone. Human rights issues are important both for individuals and the organisations that they create. As part of its commitment to the Global Compact, the business community has a responsibility to uphold human rights both in the workplace and more broadly within its sphere of influence. A growing moral imperative to behave responsibly is allied to the recognition that a good human rights record can support improved business performance.

*United Nations Global Compact,*
*"The Ten Principles," March 2008.*
*www.unglobalcompact.org.*

ing business, have human rights responsibilities. Business-led and multi-stakeholder approaches to addressing a range of thematic issues—such as labour rights violations, threats to personal security and freedom of expression, among others— are clear signs of broad agreement that human rights are "everybody's business". More and more companies are positively engaged in the effort to address challenging human rights issues, like what to do when operating in countries experiencing violent conflict, or how to do business in a "human rights aware" way even when competitors don't care or don't pay a price for doing the wrong thing. Personally, I have learned a great deal about the business case for integrating a human rights approach as part of corporate sustainability in my role as honorary Chair of the Business Leaders Initiative on Human Rights.

It is safe to say that much has changed over the past decade, and there is much to celebrate in this 60th year of the UDHR. But it is also clear that a great deal of work remains.

## Work for the Future

To start, even the most committed managers still need more practical guidance on what human rights mean for them, and how these issues can be integrated within day-to-day operations. Over the past year, I have been pleased to chair the Global Compact's Human Rights Working Group which seeks to address this challenge. Since our first meeting during the Leaders Summit last July [2007], the Working Group has made a good start in advancing the business and human rights agenda within the Global Compact. Our efforts have included engaging with the growing number of Global Compact Local Networks, identifying key human rights relevant dilemmas faced by companies, and developing a process to provide advice on practical ways of overcoming these challenges.

Many other issues require further attention beyond the immediate scope of the Global Compact. For example, although it is widely agreed that states are the primary duty bearers in relation to human rights, not enough attention has been given to the role of government in protecting against third-party abuses of rights, including by business entities, through appropriate and universally enforced national regulation. This must change if all companies—small and large, local and international are to modify their behaviors to be consistent with human rights standards. Today, far too many companies still avoid scrutiny, perhaps because they are not major brands, are not listed on major [stock] exchanges or are not in the supply chain of responsible companies. This duty of states was clearly identified by Professor John Ruggie, UN [United Nations] Special Representative on Business and Human Rights, in his 2007 report to the UN Human Rights Council.

We need to find ways to engage private and state-owned enterprises from emerging market economies; increasingly these companies are becoming important players on the global stage. Developing adequate accountability practices which ensure that promising multi-stakeholder efforts gain broad legitimacy in developing and developed economies alike is yet another area requiring renewed focus and joint action.

## A Unique Opportunity

The 60th anniversary of the Universal Declaration presents a key opportunity to address these challenges. We hope the many companies that have not thought seriously about these issues will view 2008 as the time to make commitments to human rights within their spheres of influence.

There are many ways to get involved. In cooperation with the Office of the High Commissioner for Human Rights, the Global Compact Human Rights Working Group has offered numerous concrete suggestions for actions that companies can take on the occasion of the 60th anniversary of the UDHR, including in their internal policies and practices, as well as with subsidiaries and suppliers.

The "Every Human Has Rights" 60th anniversary campaign has been launched by The Elders, a group of leaders committed to tackling some of the world's toughest problems. Nelson Mandela [former president of South Africa] and other members of The Elders are calling on each of us to make a pledge to live by the principles of the Universal Declaration. This provides an opportunity for companies to encourage their employees and wider stakeholders to learn more about human rights and take personal action.

On 10 December 2008, we will truly be able to celebrate the 60th anniversary of the Universal Declaration if concrete actions are taken in the months ahead to build a stronger international human rights regime that guides all actors in society, including business.

> *"Let's strengthen the expectations of corporations and governments by reiterating their fundamental accountability to the law, not to the CSR [corporate social responsibility] community. Businesses, governments, and NGOs [nongovernmental organizations] will continue to debate CSR, but legal compliance should not be up for debate."*

# Only Strong Laws Can Compel Corporations to Protect Human Rights

*Cheryl Marihugh*

*In this viewpoint Cheryl Marihugh who advises businesses, nongovernmental organizations, and multilateral institutions on social and environmental issues, points out that many companies are failing to comply with existing human rights laws. Because of this, she says, it is important to separate the issue of compliance with existing laws from the issue of socially responsible, "aspirational" corporate practices. Marihugh contends that allowing*

Cheryl Marihugh, "Corporate Social Responsibility: An Insider's View," *Dollars & Sense*, May–June 2006. Reproduced by permission of Dollars and Sense, a progressive economics magazine.

*the two to run together creates the impression that compliance with existing laws is a voluntary choice, when in fact, it should not be.*

As you read, consider the following questions:

1. Why does Cheryl Marihugh object to treating factory monitoring as a corporate social responsibility issue?

2. Marihugh mentions a 2005 report of an audit of eighty-eight factories. What did the audit find?

3. List some of the reasons Marihugh gives for saying that getting multinational corporations to comply with human rights laws will not be easy.

More and more companies are adopting "corporate social responsibility" (CSR) programs. Broadly, CSR programs are supposed to assess and improve corporate operations in relation to a range of values beyond profit: human rights, environmental protection, contribution to local communities, and workplace diversity among others. A central feature of many CSR programs—codes of conduct—arose in response to activism around sweatshop conditions in the factories where consumer goods are manufactured. International brands—starting in the apparel, footwear, and toy industries, but spreading to others—have adopted these codes for the factories that form their global supply chains. The codes require monitoring of such conditions as freedom of association, child labor, discrimination, harassment, wages, working hours, and health and safety, all under the rubric of CSR. No doubt it's a positive development that multinational corporations are paying some attention to these issues. But should monitoring really be part of CSR? I'm not so sure.

## Focus on Legal Requirements, Not Voluntary Measures

For several years I led a compliance program for a large footwear company, and I strongly endorse holding companies re-

sponsible for monitoring their supply chains. What I object to is placing factory monitoring under the umbrella of CSR. Most monitoring relates to compliance with labor laws. But by combining compliance with existing laws, on the one hand, and aspirational goals that go beyond existing legal mandates, on the other, CSR dilutes the incentive for companies to improve conditions. Positioning legal and regulatory topics under the CSR rubric allows them to fall into an "optional" category. Differentiating compliance with the law as a distinct expectation could strengthen the case when asking multinationals to ensure basic standards, which could be met in many countries by complying with current labor regulations.

Conferences worldwide are now marketed to contract factory owners that manufacture for international brands, with "CSR" invariably in the title. However, the sessions relate largely to labor law. While not at all intentional, this language merges what is required with what is desired.

This confusion becomes more detrimental as the debate over CSR grows. Early last year [2005], *The Economist* ran a special section on CSR. Clive Crook, a deputy editor of the magazine, expressed his skepticism of CSR in several articles. But like most CSR critics, Crook acknowledged that it is a matter of course that companies need to respect the regulatory arena. (Although regrettably, I did once hear a senior vice president state that legal compliance is essentially a "cultural" issue!) This baseline requirement typically receives a benign nod, as if compliance with existing laws and regulations is all taken care of.

In the CSR community itself, mention statutory obligations and eyes start glazing over, as if merely obeying the law is no particular challenge. But in my experience, compliance in the global outsourcing world is, in fact, quite hard. The annual report of the Fair Labor Association (FLA) illustrates this. The FLA represents a group of 20 brands that work together to improve factory conditions globally. Annual public

reports present audit findings for factories that supply the member companies, and the findings are emblematic of the global picture.

## Violations of the Law Are Too Common

The group's 2005 report presents audits of 88 factories. This small group of factories had over 1,600 violations, including 705 in health and safety, 231 in wages and benefits, 118 in working hours, 94 in overtime compensation, 81 in harassment & abuse, and 64 in freedom of association. Detailed audit reports show the majority of these to be violations not only of the FLA's code of conduct, but also of specific labor laws in each country. Moreover, the report notes that given the limitations of the audit process, violations may actually be higher than reported; for example, it acknowledges that ". . . it is likely that the rate of incidence of falsified records relating to hours and wages . . . is higher than actually reported."

Other reports have noted similar findings. The *Financial Times* covered a report issued by a European organization on the impact of global factory monitoring and noted, "Social audits of clothing factories in developing countries are failing to detect excessive and forced overtime, abusive treatment of workers and violations of freedom of association. . . ." And Anuja Mirchandaney of *The Hindu Times* cited labor law violations as a major problem in India's garment industry: "Workers are not being paid even statutory wages, as payment is linked to reaching unreasonably high production targets— simply put, unpaid overtime." In short, the global outsourcing world has a long way to go merely to attain legal compliance.

When subcontractors—even those that are subject to monitoring—still routinely violate local labor law, CSR programs and their advocates may be muddying the waters. The advocacy community presents wage demands—e.g. the demand that subcontractors pay a "living wage"—which are aspirational. But urging multinationals to pay higher wages as-

# Legislation Is More Effective than CSR

In the last decade, voluntary corporate social responsibility (CSR) strategies have become the primary means of tackling problems such as poor labour standards, aggressive marketing of products for children, and environmental harm resulting from company action or inaction. Save the Children and the Corporate Responsibility (CORE) Coalition have become increasingly concerned that, while governments around the world increasingly favour these approaches, such strategies may have only limited application. . . .

The codes have worked effectively only in instances where there has been strong government involvement through legislation and enforcement. While voluntary initiatives have made some progress in encouraging more ethical corporate practice, there are serious limitations as to what voluntarism can achieve. In spite of this, governments have been reluctant to review the efficacy of voluntary approaches, and business leaders often fail to acknowledge that legislation may in fact be a more effective means of upholding higher social and environmental standards for companies.

*Deborah Doane and Alison Holder, Executive Summary,*
*"Why Corporate Social Responsibility Is Failing Children," 2007.*
*www.corporate-responsibility.org.*

sumes that legal wages are already being paid. When wages are viewed solely as a CSR issue, critics inside and outside of companies are able to sideline the wage discussion altogether by dismissing demands for "living wages" as unrealistic.

Let's look at this situation in a real context. With its marketing strategy built on a rhetoric of "social justice," The Tim

berland Company is a multinational that plays actively in the CSR field. The company's recently released 2004 CSR report includes a breakdown of factory violations by category that closely mirrors the FLA breakdown, with "compensation (i.e., minimum wage)" the second highest category of violations (12%). By definition, violations of this part of Timberland's code of conduct constitute primarily violations of law. Timberland's CSR report claims the company is stepping up its program "from compliance to enablement." But isn't it premature to move beyond compliance when many workers are apparently not yet getting even the wages they're legally entitled to? If companies merely ensured that their suppliers obeyed the law, that could bring economic restitution to millions of workers whose pay is purposely miscalculated.

## Managers Don't Comply with Existing Laws

Unfortunately, many managers still question, or resent, the view that corporations are responsible for the compliance of their suppliers. They view monitoring as voluntary—a program that can be tweaked according to business needs. However, a legal linkage does exist through standard manufacturing contracts, which contain compliance clauses, and a recent case suggests that such contract language can have teeth. In *Doe vs. Unocal*, Burmese workers who suffered human rights abuses on a pipeline project brought suit against Unocal, which was a partner in the project. Commenting on the findings, the *Chapman Law Review* noted, "future plaintiffs seem on firm ground for pursuing corporations in federal court . . . for their human rights abuses abroad. Such plaintiffs may have even greater success pursuing comparable state claims based on state constitutional and statutory provisions forbidding forced labor, unfair competition, and unjust enrichment."

The Unocal case "shows that corporations have both direct and indirect human rights responsibilities," says Susan Aaronson, director of globalization studies at the Kenan Institute, a

Washington think tank. Today, human rights cases usually stem from extreme physical abuses, but society's concept of what constitutes "abuses" will likely continue to expand. If labor laws are consistently broken with the knowledge of business partners, this could conceivably be considered "unjust enrichment." What could separating legal compliance out from CSR do?

- Provide greater incentive for companies to focus on first keeping the law. Corporate leaders and their general counsels would give compliance issues a higher priority if they recognized the risk of increased scrutiny on the legal angle of their global operations. In Timberland's case, its sole performance indicator for monitoring is "percentage of factories assessed." If the company were mandated to report legal compliance, this would be a much stronger indicator of actual working conditions.

- Give greater accuracy to CSR ratings. Company CSR assessment questionnaires frequently put more emphasis on aspirational issues. While legal compliance is also included, it is not meaningfully probed. The socially responsible investment community would do well to separate out legal requirements and form one assessment on these, and then evaluate a company on "beyond compliance" issues.

- Support company compliance staff, who must often make unpopular requests. In the experience of many staff, it seems as if upper management must be persuaded to support not only CSR goals, but regulatory recommendations as well, e.g., factory reimbursement of workers who were not paid legally.

- Increase the number of companies engaged in these issues. If companies regard factory monitoring as a po-

tential legal liability, they are more likely to attend to it whether or not they have a penchant for CSR.

Getting multinationals and their subcontractors to comply with local labor laws won't be easy. Many countries, north and south, do not direct sufficient resources to enforcement. Management practices that evade regulations persist. Furthermore, labor laws can indeed be difficult to interpret. But suppliers, companies, and countries can't point to these difficulties to elude legal accountability. Legal compliance will be hard to achieve, whether within the CSR rubric or not, but extracting legal compliance from CSR has the advantage of bringing to light a range of workplace and wage issues that companies are required by law to attend to.

In the face of CSR's ongoing controversy, let's strengthen the expectations of corporations and governments by reiterating their fundamental accountability to the law, not to the CSR community. Businesses, governments, and NGOs [nongovernmental organizations] will continue to debate CSR, but legal compliance should not be up for debate.

> *"Our focus should be on ways to reduce or compensate for the governance gaps created by globalization, because they permit corporate-related human rights harm to occur even where none may be intended."*

# The UN's Framework for Business and Human Rights Seeks to Fill the Governance Gap Caused by Globalization

*John Ruggie*

*John Ruggie is the Kirkpatrick Professor of International Affairs at Harvard University. In this viewpoint, written in his role as Special Representative of the United Nations (UN) Secretary-General on the issue of human rights, transnational corporations and other business enterprises, he argues that a "governance gap" created by globalization means that many human rights concerns are not being adequately addressed. The United Nation's framework for business and human rights, which asserts the responsibility of states and corporations, respectively, to protect and respect human rights, and to provide remedies for human rights*

John Ruggie, "Protect, Respect and Remedy: A Framework for Business and Human Rights," www.mitpressjournals.org/doi/pdf/10.1162/itgg.20083.2.189, Reproduced by permission of The MIT Press, Cambridge, MA.

*abuses, is a necessary measure, he says. Ruggie asserts that the UN, despite lacking authority apart from the will of its member nations, has an important role to play in creating an international culture of respect for human rights.*

As you read, consider the following questions:

1. According to the author, what is the main cause of most corporate-related human rights abuses that occur today?

2. What are the three core principles outlined in the UN framework for business and human rights?

3. According to the author, what basic challenge do the three core principles of the framework seek to address?

The international community is still in the early stages of adapting the human rights regime to provide more effective protection to individuals and communities against corporate-related human rights harm. This report to the Human Rights Council presents a principles-based conceptual and policy framework intended to help achieve this aim.

Business is the major source of investment and job creation, and markets can be highly efficient means for allocating scarce resources. They constitute powerful forces capable of generating economic growth, reducing poverty, and increasing demand for the rule of law, thereby contributing to the realization of a broad spectrum of human rights. But markets work optimally only if they are embedded within rules, customs, and institutions. Markets themselves require these to survive and thrive, while society needs them to manage the adverse effects of market dynamics and produce the public goods that markets undersupply. Indeed, history teaches us that markets pose the greatest risks—to society and business itself—when their scope and power far exceed the reach of the institutional underpinnings that allow them to function smoothly and ensure their political sustainability. This is such

a time, and escalating charges of corporate-related human rights abuses are the canary in the coal mine, signalling that all is not well.

The root cause of the business and human rights predicament today lies in the governance gaps created by globalization—between the scope and impact of economic forces and actors, and the capacity of societies to manage their adverse consequences. These governance gaps provide the permissive environment for wrongful acts by companies of all kinds without adequate sanctioning or reparation. How to narrow and ultimately bridge the gaps in relation to human rights is our fundamental challenge. . . .

The business and human rights debate currently lacks an authoritative focal point. Claims and counter-claims proliferate, initiatives abound, and yet no effort reaches significant scale. Amid this confusing mix, laggards—States as well as companies—continue to fly below the radar.

Some stakeholders believe that the solution lies in a limited list of human rights for which companies would have responsibility, while extending to companies, where they have influence, essentially the same range of responsibilities as States. For reasons this report spells out, the Special Representative has not adopted this formula. Briefly, business can affect virtually all internationally recognized rights. Therefore, any limited list will almost certainly miss one or more rights that may turn out to be significant in a particular instance, thereby providing misleading guidance. At the same time, as economic actors, companies have unique responsibilities. If those responsibilities are entangled with State obligations, it makes it difficult if not impossible to tell who is responsible for what in practice. Hence, this report pursues the more promising path of addressing the specific responsibilities of companies in relation to all rights they may impact.

There is no single silver bullet solution to the institutional misalignments in the business and human rights domain. In-

stead, all social actors—States, businesses, and civil society—must learn to do many things differently. But those things must cohere and become cumulative, which makes it critically important to get the foundation right.

Every stakeholder group, despite their other differences, has expressed the urgent need for a common conceptual and policy framework, a foundation on which thinking and action can build. Drawing on the mandate's work in its first two years, the Special Representative introduced the elements of a framework in multi-stakeholder consultations during the autumn of 2007.

The framework rests on differentiated but complementary responsibilities. It comprises three core principles: the State duty to protect against human rights abuses by third parties, including business; the corporate responsibility to respect human rights; and the need for more effective access to remedies. Each principle is an essential component of the framework: the State duty to protect because it lies at the very core of the international human rights regime; the corporate responsibility to respect because it is the basic expectation society has of business; and access to remedy, because even the most concerted efforts cannot prevent all abuse, while access to judicial redress is often problematic, and non-judicial means are limited in number, scope, and effectiveness. The three principles form a complementary whole in that each supports the others in achieving sustainable progress. . . .

## The Challenge

How should we frame today's challenges in order to capture their essential attributes? As noted at the outset, our focus should be on ways to reduce or compensate for the governance gaps created by globalization, because they permit corporate-related human rights harm to occur even where none may be intended.

Take the case of transnational corporations. Their legal rights have been expanded significantly over the past generation. This has encouraged investment and trade flows, but it has also created instances of imbalances between firms and States that may be detrimental to human rights. The more than 2,500 bilateral investment treaties currently in effect are a case in point. While providing legitimate protection to foreign investors, these treaties also permit those investors to take host States to binding international arbitration, including for alleged damages resulting from implementation of legislation to improve domestic social and environmental standards—even when the legislation applies uniformly to all businesses, foreign and domestic. A European mining company operating in South Africa recently challenged that country's black economic empowerment laws on these grounds.

At the same time, the legal framework regulating transnational corporations operates much as it did long before the recent wave of globalization. A parent company and its subsidiaries continue to be construed as distinct legal entities. Therefore, the parent company is generally not liable for wrongs committed by a subsidiary, even where it is the sole shareholder, unless the subsidiary is under such close operational control by the parent that it can be seen as its mere agent. Furthermore, despite the transformative changes in the global economic landscape generated by offshore sourcing, purchasing goods and services even from sole suppliers remains an unrelated party transaction. Factors such as these make it exceedingly difficult to hold the extended enterprise accountable for human rights harm.

Each legally distinct corporate entity is subject to the laws of the countries in which it is based and operates. Yet States, particularly some developing countries, may lack the institutional capacity to enforce national laws and regulations against transnational firms doing business in their territory even when the will is there, or they may feel constrained from doing so

by having to compete internationally for investment. Home States of transnational firms may be reluctant to regulate against overseas harm by these firms because the permissible scope of national regulation with extraterritorial effect remains poorly understood, or out of concern that those firms might lose investment opportunities or relocate their headquarters.

This dynamic is hardly limited to transnational corporations. To attract investments and promote exports, governments may exempt national firms from certain legal and regulatory requirements or fail to adopt such standards in the first place.

And what is the result? In his 2006 report, the Special Representative surveyed allegations of the worst cases of corporate-related human rights harm. They occurred, predictably, where governance challenges were greatest: disproportionately in low-income countries; in countries that often had just emerged from or still were in conflict; and in countries where the rule of law was weak and levels of corruption high. A significant fraction of the allegations involved companies being complicit in the acts of governments or armed factions. A recent study conducted for the mandate by the Office of the United Nations High Commissioner for Human Rights (OHCHR) confirms these findings but also shows that adverse business impacts on human rights are not limited to these contexts.

## The Framework

Insofar as governance gaps are at the root of the business and human rights predicament, effective responses must aim to reduce those gaps. But individual actions, whether by States or firms, may be too constrained by the competitive dynamics just described. Therefore, more coherent and concerted approaches are required. The framework of "protect, respect, and remedy" can assist all social actors—governments, companies,

and civil society—to reduce the adverse human rights consequences of these misalignments.

Take first the State duty to protect. It has both legal and policy dimensions. As documented in the Special Representative's 2007 report, international law provides that States have a duty to protect against human rights abuses by non-State actors, including by business, affecting persons within their territory or jurisdiction. To help States interpret how this duty applies under the core United Nations human rights conventions, the treaty monitoring bodies generally recommend that States take all necessary steps to protect against such abuse, including to prevent, investigate, and punish the abuse, and to provide access to redress. States have discretion to decide what measures to take, but the treaty bodies indicate that both regulation and adjudication of corporate activities vis-à-vis human rights are appropriate. They also suggest that the duty applies to the activities of all types of businesses—national and transnational, large and small—and that it applies to all rights private parties are capable of impairing. Regional human rights systems have reached similar conclusions.

Experts disagree on whether international law requires home States to help prevent human rights abuses abroad by corporations based within their territory. There is greater consensus that those States are not prohibited from doing so where a recognized basis of jurisdiction exists, and the actions of the home State meet an overall reasonableness test, which includes non-intervention in the internal affairs of other States. Indeed, there is increasing encouragement at the international level, including from the treaty bodies, for home States to take regulatory action to prevent abuse by their companies overseas.

The 2007 report also described the expanding web of potential corporate liability for international crimes, reflecting international standards but imposed through national courts. As discussed in the next section, in some jurisdictions, inno-

# Mandate of the UN Special Representative on Business & Human Rights

The UN [United Nations] Commission on Human Rights originally adopted a resolution on 20 April 2005 requesting "the Secretary-General to appoint a special representative on the issue of human rights and transnational corporations and other business enterprises". The UN Human Rights Council renewed the Special Representative's term on 18 June 2008, by a resolution that included the following [partial] mandate:

"(a) To provide views and concrete and practical re-commendations on ways to strengthen the fulfilment of the duty of the State to protect all human rights from abuses by or involving transnational corporations and other business enterprises, including through inter-national cooperation;

(b) To elaborate further on the scope and content of the corporate responsibility to respect all human rights and to provide concrete guidance to business and other stakeholders;

(c) To explore options and make recommendations, at the national, regional and international level, for enhan-cing access to effective remedies available to those whose human rights are impacted by corporate activities;

(d) To integrate a gender perspective throughout his work and to give special attention to persons belonging to vulnerable groups, in particular children;" . . .

*"Mandate of the UN Special Representative on Business & Human Rights,"* Business & Human Rights Resource Centre, *July 26, 2008. Reproduced by permission.*

vations in regulation and adjudication are moving toward greater recognition of the complex organizational forms characteristic of modern business enterprises.

Further refinements of the legal understanding of the State duty to protect by authoritative bodies at national and international levels are highly desirable. But even within existing legal principles, the policy dimensions of the duty to protect require increased attention and more imaginative approaches from States.

It is often stressed that governments are the appropriate entities to make the difficult balancing decisions required to reconcile different societal needs. However, the Special Representative's work raises questions about whether governments have got the balance right. His consultations and research, including a questionnaire survey sent to all Member States, indicate that many governments take a narrow approach to managing the business and human rights agenda. It is often segregated within its own conceptual and (typically weak) institutional box—kept apart from, or heavily discounted in, other policy domains that shape business practices, including commercial policy, investment policy, securities regulation, and corporate governance. This inadequate domestic policy coherence is replicated internationally. Governments should not assume they are helping business by failing to provide adequate guidance for, or regulation of, the human rights impact of corporate activities. On the contrary, the less governments do, the more they increase reputational and other risks to business.

The corporate responsibility to respect human rights is the second principle. It is recognized in such soft law instruments as the Tripartite Declaration of Principles Concerning Multinational Enterprises and Social Policy, and the OECD Guidelines for Multinational Enterprises. It is invoked by the largest global business organizations in their submission to the mandate, which states that companies "are expected to obey the law, even if it is not enforced, and to respect the principles of

relevant international instruments where national law is absent." It is one of the commitments companies undertake in joining the Global Compact. And the Special Representative's surveys document the fact that companies worldwide increasingly claim they respect human rights.

To respect rights essentially means not to infringe on the rights of others—put simply, to do no harm. Because companies can affect virtually all internationally recognized rights, they should consider the responsibility to respect in relation to all such rights, although some may require greater attention in particular contexts. There are situations in which companies may have additional responsibilities—for example, where they perform certain public functions, or because they have undertaken additional commitments voluntarily. But the responsibility to respect is the baseline expectation for all companies in all situations.

Yet how do companies know they respect human rights? Do they have systems in place enabling them to support the claim with any degree of confidence? Most do not. What is required is due diligence—a process whereby companies not only ensure compliance with national laws but also manage the risk of human rights harm with a view to avoiding it. The scope of human rights related due diligence is determined by the context in which a company is operating, its activities, and the relationships associated with those activities.

Access to remedy is the third principle. Even where institutions operate optimally, disputes over the human rights impact of companies are likely to occur. Currently, access to formal judicial systems is often most difficult where the need is greatest. And non-judicial mechanisms are seriously underdeveloped—from the company level up through national and international levels. . . .

## The Task Ahead

The current debate on the business and human rights agenda originated in the 1990s, as liberalization, technology, and in-

novations in corporate structure combined to expand prior limits on where and how businesses could operate globally. Many countries, including in the developing world, have been able to take advantage of this new economic landscape to increase prosperity and reduce poverty. But as has happened throughout history, rapid market expansion has also created governance gaps in numerous policy domains: gaps between the scope of economic activities and actors, and the capacity of political institutions to manage their adverse consequences. The area of business and human rights is one such domain.

In fact, progress has been made in the past decade, at least in some industries and by growing numbers of firms. The Special Representative's 2007 report detailed novel multi-stakeholder initiatives, public-private hybrids combining mandatory with voluntary measures, and industry and company self-regulation. All have their strengths and shortcomings, but few would have been conceivable a mere decade ago. Likewise, there is an expanding web of potential corporate liability for international crimes, reflecting international standards but imposed through national courts. Governments have adopted a variety of measures, albeit gingerly to date, to promote a corporate culture respectful of human rights. Fragments of international institutional provisions exist with similar aims.

Without in any manner disparaging these steps, our fundamental problem is that there are too few of them, none has reached a scale commensurate with the challenges at hand, there is little cross-learning, and they do not cohere as parts of a more systemic response with cumulative effects. That is what needs fixing. And that is what the framework of "protect, respect and remedy" is intended to help achieve.

The United Nations is not a centralized command-and-control system that can impose its will on the world—indeed it has no "will" apart from that with which Member States endow it. But it can and must lead intellectually and by setting expectations and aspirations. The Human Rights Council can

make a singular contribution to closing the governance gaps in business and human rights by supporting this framework, inviting its further elaboration, and fostering its uptake by all relevant social actors.

> *"Instead of fostering a corporate culture in which boards of directors develop the best balance between their monitoring of human rights compliance by the corporation and advising management as to strategy, the Report's proposed pressures would force directors to navigate a maze of procedural imperatives and 'evolving' best practices."*

# The UN's Framework for Business and Human Rights Requires Too Much of Corporations

*Martin Lipton and Kevin S. Schwartz*

*Martin Lipton and Kevin S. Schwartz are attorneys with Wachtell, Lipton, Rosen & Katz, a law firm that specializes in business law, including mergers and acquisitions. In this viewpoint they argue that, although the United Nations' proposed framework for business and human rights advances the discussion of how to harness globalization's benefits while redressing and eliminating gaps that permit the abuse of human rights, it unfairly makes*

Martin Lipton and Kevin S. Schwartz, "A United Nations Proposal Defining Corporate Social Responsibility for Human Rights," *The AMLaw Daily*, May 1, 2008. Reproduced by permission of Wachtell, Lipton, Rosen & Katz.

*corporations responsible for political, civil, economic, and social deficiencies of the countries in which they do business. They maintain that the framework for business and human rights imposes on corporations responsibilities that properly belong to the states, and exposes corporations to great liability for human rights conditions over which they have little control.*

As you read, consider the following questions:

1. What kinds of companies are covered by the recent United Nations report on businesses' responsibilities with respect to human rights?

2. Do you agree or disagree that global corporations should have to complete human rights impact assessments in order to do business?

3. According to the authors, what are some of the negative consequences businesses could face if the recommendations of the United Nations Special Representative's Report are implemented?

The social responsibility of corporations has been a growing issue over the past 50 years. The United Nations has emerged as a central forum in this debate and has focused attention on the scope of businesses' responsibilities concerning human rights. Leading this effort, a Special Representative to the Secretary-General recently completed a report with broad implications for global business and particularly for companies that operate on a global basis, in emerging markets, in underdeveloped countries, or in countries that lack a democratic system.

The Special Representative's Report, which will be considered ... by the United Nations [UN] Human Rights Council, proposes that corporations bear the "responsibility to respect human rights," that the State has a "duty to protect" against human rights abuses by companies, and that both the State and businesses must provide more effective access to remedies

for human rights violations. Despite the assurance that corporations' duty to respect human rights "essentially means not to infringe on the rights of others—put simply, to do no harm," the framework recommended to the United Nations could impose on businesses an array of expansive obligations that require close attention by corporate management and boards. To discharge their responsibility to respect human rights, corporations would be required to conduct a broad due diligence process "to become aware of, prevent and address adverse human rights impacts," purportedly in the same way as corporations already must "assess and manage financial and related risks."

The effect of this proposal would be to impose on corporations the obligation to compensate for the political, civil, economic, social, or other deficiencies of the countries in which they conduct business. Further, corporate boards of directors may even be expected to monitor and ensure the vindication of broad-textured principles enshrined in various international human rights instruments. The following sets forth the core principles which the U.N. Human Rights Council may endorse to guide corporate responsibilities for human rights and additionally considers their implications for directors. Corporations and their boards should carefully weigh the consequences of this development in the corporate social responsibility debate.

## Protect, Respect and Remedy

Under the Special Representative's proposal to the U.N. Human Rights Council, the corporate responsibility to respect human rights would require a process of due diligence that ensures compliance with national laws but also manages the risks of human rights harms in order to avoid them. To meet their due diligence obligation, companies would be expected to: (a) establish a human rights policy, (b) integrate the policy as a key factor in decision-making throughout company man-

agement systems, (c) conduct human rights "impact assessments" in order "to understand how existing and proposed activities may affect human rights," and (d) track and respond to their performance. Importantly, the responsibility to respect human rights also would require the establishment of effective "means for those who believe they have been harmed to bring this to the attention of the company and seek remediation, without prejudice to legal channels available."

The responsibilities involved in a human rights impact assessment warrant particular scrutiny. The Report only briefly addresses the shape of an impact assessment but specifies that it should take place before significant project activity begins and, "[b]ased on the information uncovered, companies should refine their plans to address and avoid potential negative human rights impacts on an ongoing basis." According to a more detailed methodological report which the Special Representative submitted to the U.N. Human Rights Council in 2007, a human rights impact assessment would include the following components:

1. A description of the proposed business activity;

2. A catalogue of the legal, regulatory and administrative frameworks to which the activity is subject, as well as the international human rights frameworks that apply to the area in which the business will operate;

3. A description of the human rights conditions in the area surrounding the business activity before significant activity begins;

4. A statement of what is likely to change because of the business activity, which may include identifying multiple scenarios or predicting outcomes based on varying levels of intervention. Relevant factors include country-specific human rights challenges as well as the potential human rights impact of the company's activities and of the relationships associated with those activities;

5. A prioritization of the human rights challenges for the company;

6. A management plan that includes both recommendations to address identified human rights challenges and provisions for the monitoring of baseline indicators.

As standard practice, human rights impact assessments "would always be published in full," but "reasonable" political, legal, or security risks "must also be considered and may force a partial or summary publication." Companies would be expected to implement—and respond to—monitoring and auditing processes that provide regular updates on the business activity's human rights impact.

Finally, the Special Representative's Report proposes that a business's evaluation of its human rights impact and performance should be measured, "at a minimum," according to the substantive "benchmarks" of international human rights instruments like the Universal Declaration of Human Rights and the International Covenants on Civil and Political Rights and on Economic, Social and Cultural Rights.

The expansive procedural imperatives and the substantive standard proposed by the Special Representative would impose on corporations sweeping duties to compensate for deficiencies which a State has been unable, or unwilling, to address in the political, civil, economic, social, or other systems of the areas in which business activities will take place. In particular, officers and directors should consider three specific consequences.

First, the proposal of international rights conventions as the substantive standard for the due diligence process would impose on corporations the State's responsibility—but not its power and legitimacy—to vindicate the broad-textured guarantees of international human rights instruments according to local circumstances.

Second, the measure of a corporate activity's human rights impact would be tied inextricably to deficiencies in the politi-

## The Global Compact, Human Rights and the Environment

At a time when deep divergences have emerged on how best to address the major challenges facing the world and the ability of the United Nations to deal with them is being questioned, the Global Compact has become an important rallying point for the support of internationally agreed basic values.

With more than 1200 companies from more than 70 countries North and South—from businesses with a global reach to small and medium-size enterprises—having responded positively to the Secretary-General's call to promote shared values in the areas of human rights, labor relations and the environment, a momentum has developed that promises increasing support for this groundbreaking initiative. . . .

Experience with the Global Compact to date demonstrates the importance of adhering to its original concept—aspirational and exhortative in nature, encouraging continuous improvement in business behavior, and serving as a learning forum through the dissemination of good company practices in the fields covered by the Compact's principles. . . .

The Global Compact's greatest strength lies in its voluntary nature, which acts as a powerful complement to the necessary action by governments themselves to safeguard and advance its principles.

*"The Global Compact: A Business Perspective,"*
Global Compact Leaders Summit,
*June 24, 2004. Reproduced by permission.*

cal, civil, economic, or social conditions left unaddressed by the State. In fact, one U.N. Discussion Paper proposed that

the human rights impact assessment must evaluate "the state of realization of a broad spectrum of rights rather than only those obviously impacted by the proposed business activity."

Third, the burden imposed on companies to predict outcomes and "prioritize" human rights challenges, in ways allegedly comparable to financial and other risk management strategies, would expose businesses to enormous liability. Indeed, this is readily apparent from an earlier report to the U.N. Human Rights Council in which the Special Representative acknowledged that stating a project's likely impact is a "difficult and subjective exercise." The report noted that in predicting outcomes, a human rights impact assessment actually might have to look beyond a project's likely effects to consider as well "community perceptions of what is likely to change; even though a new petrochemicals plant might produce no local pollution, community fears about air or water quality will necessitate action by the company." Whatever the good-faith efforts applied by corporations, these far-reaching process requirements for respecting rights would furnish any number of liability claims, whether based on erroneous predictions of possible human rights outcomes, a board's decision not to follow every recommendation in an impact assessment's management plan, or a company's "prioritization" of human rights challenges and corresponding project designs.

## The State Duty to Protect

Directors also should take particular note of the Report's focus on the State duty to protect against human rights abuses by businesses. The Special Representative urges States to improve their protection against corporate human rights abuses by fostering corporate cultures in which respect for rights is an essential part of doing business. The Report suggests that one way to exert market pressures on companies to cultivate such a corporate culture would be to expand fiduciary duties to include the obligation to consider the human rights impact of corporate activities. Lest this dramatic expansion of board

monitoring duties appear to be an unlikely development, consider two recent expressions of this reform trend.

Following a process safety accident that occurred in 2005 in BP's Texas City refinery, an independent panel led by former Secretary of State James A. Baker III was established to review the company's corporate safety culture, management systems and oversight, and to make recommendations to improve BP's process safety performance. In a report describing the "evolving" understanding of the role of boards of directors in health and safety matters, the independent panel noted the United Kingdom Health and Safety Commission's recommendation that the board of directors "needs to accept formally and publicly its collective role in providing health and safety leadership in its organisation." The panel urged that, in pursuit of best practices, directors' role in governing the process safety issues in their business "should be supported by formal individual terms of reference, covering as a minimum setting process safety policy and strategy development, setting standards, performance monitoring and internal control." Such an expansion of the monitoring and oversight obligations of boards would mark a significant change in the distribution of responsibilities in corporations.

Moreover, to demonstrate how States can increase the pressure on companies to respect human rights, the Special Representative's Report specifically references the binding legal obligations which British law began imposing on directors by "redefining fiduciary duties." Under Section 172 of the United Kingdom's Companies Act 2006, for directors to act in good faith to promote the success of their company they must "have regard" to "the impact of the company's operations on the community and the environment." In fact, during its consideration by Parliament, an earlier version of the legislation had attributed this new responsibility to directors only "so far as reasonably practicable," but the Government removed this reasonableness clause before final passage of the law. To the extent the U.K. Companies Act forms one of the bases on which

the U.N. Human Rights Council may endorse the State's duty to protect against human rights abuses, such a new legal standard would mark a dramatic expansion beyond traditional constituency statutes. Further, even if the U.N. Human Rights Council does not specifically address the redefining of fiduciary duties or best practices, the Special Representative's Report reflects a trend in reform proposals to which corporations and boards may wish to respond.

Instead of fostering a corporate culture in which boards of directors develop the best balance between their monitoring of human rights compliance by the corporation and advising management as to strategy, the Report's proposed pressures would force directors to navigate a maze of procedural imperatives and "evolving" best practices. An expansion of fiduciary duties would make the work of boards of directors more difficult without yielding a correlative improvement in the targeted corporate focus on human rights. In particular, a challenge which boards must confront is the procedural focus that animates the Special Representative's definition of respect for human rights. The proposal places a premium on broad process duties—from the due diligence obligation of human rights impact assessments, to the board monitoring of corporate compliance—but these should not form the anchor of corporations' social responsibility to respect human rights. To be sure, procedural attention to potential human rights harms before they occur, and throughout the lifecycle of a business project, can provide valuable safeguards for human rights, but the Special Representative's Report goes much further. Consequently, directors must cautiously evaluate the repercussions of the Special Representative's proposal, for corporate boards and for global business more generally.

## Moving the Discussion Forward

The Report of the Special Representative marks an important development in the global debate over corporate social responsibility. It advances the discussion of how we may better

harness globalization's benefits while redressing and eliminating the gaps that permit the abuse of human rights. It also advances the cause of social responsibility activists who propose proxy resolutions and take other actions to pressure companies. Experience shows that these proposals resonate most strongly with public pension funds and in the academic community with pressure on endowments to disinvest securities of companies that are not responsive to the activists' proposals.

The Report bears significant, potentially harmful implications for global business and for meaningful accountability in various social actors' duties to fulfill the promises of international human rights instruments. The proposal to the U.N. Human Rights Council thus requires close scrutiny by the business community. The Report will invite immense pressure on corporations and their directors, and boards should work closely with management to address this development through a special committee or a public affairs committee.

# Periodical Bibliography

*The following articles have been selected to supplement the diverse views presented in this chapter.*

Alicia Barney — "Cleaner Karats," *Newsweek*, March 12, 2007.

*The Economist* — "Doing the Wrong Thing; Business and Human Rights," October 27, 2007.

*Food & Beverage Close-Up* — "The Coca-Cola Company Joins Initiative on Human Rights," August 24, 2007.

Jeremy Gaunt — "DAVOS: Rocker Peter Gabriel Wants 'You Tube for Human Rights,'" *Information Week*, January 2007.

Steve Hendershot — "Villain, Hero or Something Else? Abbott Laboratories' Charitable Balancing Act," *Crain's Chicago Business*, August 20, 2007.

*Institutional Investor International Edition* — "Responsible Behavior Creates Value for Shareholders and Improves Bottom Line," June 2006.

*Investment News* — "Educate Clients on New Socially Conscious Offerings," April 21, 2008.

Georg Kell, Anne-Marie Slaughter, and Thomas Hale — "Silent Reform Through the Global Compact," *UN Chronicle*, March 2007.

Rachel Mendleson — "Your Bling Can Save the World," *Maclean's*, June 23, 2008.

Sheri Qualters — "Rights Cases Multiply Against Companies," *Fulton County Daily Report*, August 24, 2007.

Mark Taylor — "Companies Should Obey the Law in Lawless Lands," *The Lawyer*, May 19, 2008.

Marianne Wilson — "Doing Good Is More than a Feel-Good Option," *Chain Store Age*, October 2005.

OPPOSING
VIEWPOINTS®
SERIES

# CHAPTER 4

# What Factors Are Influencing Corporations to Behave More Responsibly?

# Chapter Preface

Paul Hawken's, book *The Ecology of Commerce*, inspired Ray C. Anderson, the CEO of Interface Corporation, to redesign the workflows at his firm. In his book, Hawkens argued that in an age of ecological crisis, commerce needs to become a system of creative and restorative processes. "The key," he wrote, "is to inspire a willing, uncoerced, even joyous redesign of the way we conduct business."

After reading *The Ecology of Commerce*, Anderson became convinced that the kind of restorative economy Hawkens envisioned was a goal worth pursuing. Interface, which manufactures modular and broadloom floor coverings for residential and commercial uses, is an example of a firm that has gone to great lengths to transform itself, to research, develop, and adopt sustainable manufacturing processes, and to build corporate social responsibility into its brand identity. "If we're successful," Anderson said in the late 1990s, "we'll spend the rest of our days harvesting yester-year's carpets and other petrochemically derived products, and recycling them into new materials; and converting sunlight into energy; with zero scrap going to the landfill and zero emissions into the ecosystem."

Many factors at work in the world today influence companies to adopt more socially responsible business models. Ideas and information travel at the speed of light. The Internet, which speeds the dissemination of new technologies and multiplies the power of marketing communications, also increases the damage that can be caused by bad press that results from human rights and environmental violations. In an era of globalism, corporations, once they become multinational, are less easily constrained by laws and regulations, but more vulnerable to public opinion and public pressure to conform to evolving standards of conduct. Educational institutions have the power to reshape curricula, and influence what is learned

by young professionals. Corporate codes of conduct, while voluntary, still have the power to influence public expectations.

The viewpoints in this chapter explore a variety of paths individuals and organizations are taking in their efforts to influence the development of a more socially responsive global business culture.

> "Despite . . . skepticism, voluntary corporate codes may improve corporate behavior even without the coercion that backs up government regulation. Companies do care about their reputations. Reputations are increasingly going global, leaving corporations increasingly vulnerable to new pressures."

# Voluntary Codes of Conduct May Provide Motivation for Responsible Corporate Behavior

*Ann Florini*

*Ann Florini is a senior fellow in the area of foreign policy with the Brookings Institution. In this viewpoint, she argues that corporate governance issues have grown complicated in the era of globalization. As transportation and communications technologies have given businesses global reach, the balance of power has shifted from national governments to corporations. Corporate affiliates have proliferated. In the complex global business environment, Florini notes that it has become difficult to effectively*

Ann Florini, "Business and Global Governance: The Growing Role of Corporate Codes of Conduct," *The Brookings Institution*, Spring 2003. Reproduced by permission.

*regulate business to protect workers, communities, and the environment. Voluntary codes of conduct are one response to this problem. Florini says that codes of conduct provide some motivation for corporations to adopt socially responsible practices in the areas of labor, the environment, and human rights.*

As you read, consider the following questions:

1. How has the relationship between businesses and governments changed in the era of globalization, according to this viewpoint?
2. According to the author, why might national regulation fall short of ensuring that national standards are met?
3. What is the difference between an aspirational code of conduct and one that is externally monitored?

These are, in many ways, halcyon days for global business. In a vast ideological shift in the late 20th century, markets rather than governments came to be seen as the road to prosperity. Governments that once nationalized foreign firms now seek out the investment, technology, and managerial expertise such companies can bring. The halls of the United Nations [UN] used to ring with calls for international regulation of those dreaded evil-doers, the multinational corporations. Now the UN instead implores business to join with it in a voluntary Global Compact to ensure respect for internationally agreed environmental, labor, and human rights standards.

And business has truly gone global. Surging transportation and communications technologies in the past few decades have encouraged firms the world over to cross borders, and revitalized industries in Europe and Japan have offered new competition to U.S. firms. At the beginning of the 1990s, some 35,000 parent multinational corporations had roughly 170,000 foreign affiliates. By the end of the decade, 60,000 parent companies had more than 500,000 foreign affiliates, accounting for a quarter of global output in the late 1990s. As

transnationals reorganize the production of goods and services, production itself is becoming global in structure.

But there are clouds on the global business horizon that go beyond the current dour economic climate. The lack of effective international (and often national) regulation to protect workers, communities, and the environment has spurred the development of a powerful movement aimed at promoting corporate social responsibility, whose partisans have on occasion forced significant changes in business practices through campaigns aimed at consumers and investors. And because unregulated business activities can cause societies to question the legitimacy of corporations, corporate leaders themselves are struggling with fundamental questions about how far their social responsibilities extend: to shareholders, employees, local communities where they operate, humanity as a whole, future generations?

## National Regulation?

Repeated efforts, starting with the proposed International Trade Organization in the 1940s, to create internationally agreed rules to regulate cross-border business have all failed. Regulation of these firms thus falls to national governments. But governments are often finding it difficult to cope. Megacompanies' huge resources dwarf those of national prosecutors, making legal control a challenge. Changes in the ways global corporations produce goods also complicate national regulation. Companies both big and small contract out with suppliers in far-flung parts of the world—Disney reputedly has some 300,000 separate suppliers. A company with a brand name such as Levi Strauss or WalMart effectively controls a long chain of frequently shifting suppliers based primarily in low-wage countries, thus controlling much of what suppliers do: what product quality standards and schedules must be met, what products will be produced. But for the most part, control over such matters as working conditions in and envi-

ronmental spillovers from those suppliers' facilities remains in the hands of the national governments where suppliers are located. Because enforcement of labor and environmental standards in those low-wage countries is often, to put it mildly, less than fully effective, this pattern of production enables rich-country firms to reap the benefits of low production costs without having to pay attention to the associated social costs.

## A Determined Company Can Flout the Law

Even in countries with well-established regulatory systems and effective courts, a determined company can flout the law. Some get caught, but only after doing extensive damage. Louisiana-Pacific Corporation was recently assessed the largest criminal fine in the 28-year history of the U.S. Clean Air Act. The company, which employs some 13,000 people in the United States, Canada, and Ireland and grossed $2.5 billion in sales in 1997, pleaded guilty to 18 felonies and agreed to pay $37 million in penalties and $5.5 million for criminal violations of the Clean Air Act.

The corporation was caught only because a former company supervisor filed a lawsuit against it alleging that he had been fired for refusing to tamper with one facility's pollution monitoring equipment. That is a rather haphazard way to regulate, but federal and state environmental officials cannot possibly closely supervise the vast array of firms operating in the United States.

National regulation, where it exists, falls far short. Many governments seem unable or unwilling to ensure that national standards exist and are adequately enforced. No matter how much corporations may complain (sometimes justifiably) about the heavy hand of government regulation, the market side has the upper hand.

To fill the governance gap, an extraordinary variety of nongovernmental groups has sprung up. Activist groups are

proving adept at shaming or coercing corporations into paying attention to what activists say are the broader social responsibilities of the private sector. And some in the corporate
world seem to be listening.

## Corporate Codes: Cover-Up, Try-Out, or Buy-In?

During the late 1970s corporations began to face nongovernmental pressures to change the way they saw their role in the
world. Principles and codes of conduct began appearing,
mostly among U.S. companies responding to waves of bad
publicity from revelations that some had been paying bribes
overseas—a practice banned by the 1977 U.S. Foreign Corrupt
Practices Act.

As corporate cross-border activity blossomed, new campaigns demanded change in corporate practices on everything
from worker rights to environmental sustainability. By the
1990s, a new "corporate social responsibility" movement was
in full swing. Corporations began learning that failing to comply with consumer and investor preferences about their behavior can be costly.

Today many companies are creating "codes of conduct"
that go beyond what local law requires. The codes are meant
to protect company reputations and reassure consumers that
their production processes are environmentally benign and
that working conditions are decent.

Sometimes governments encourage the code-of-conduct
trend. In the United States, the Clinton White House set up
an Apparel Industry Partnership that put forward a code of
conduct setting standards for working conditions, applicable
not only to participating companies but also to their foreign
contractors. Business associations have also gotten in on the
act. In 1990 the International Chamber of Commerce set
forth a Business Charter for Sustainable Development that has
since been signed by more than 2,500 companies worldwide.

But the big push for such codes has come from civil society groups, whose intense public criticism of corporate behavior can drive away customers and investors if left unanswered. Their spotlight has shone even on firms that consider themselves socially progressive. Starbucks Coffee, faced with intense picketing by activists denouncing conditions at the Guatemalan coffee plantations where it purchases beans, eventually issued a code of conduct and action plans for all its suppliers.

## Everybody Has One

By now, almost every self-respecting large corporation has a code of conduct. But the codes are highly controversial. Proponents generally see them as a valuable way to get corporations to buy into new norms of behavior without the need for government intervention, making them attractive to corporate leaders who want to fend off government regulation. More ambitious proponents see them as a means of gradually achieving consensus around standards of behavior that can be tried out voluntarily, then eventually adopted and enforced by governments. Detractors portray them as mere fig leaves.

Corporate codes are of two sorts. The first is "aspirational"—a general statement of what corporations aim to do. The Caux Principles, put forward by the Caux Roundtable, a group of senior executives from leading firms based in Europe, Japan, and the United States, are a good example. They consist of general principles, broad to the point of mushiness (corporations should operate in a spirit of honesty and fairness, should contribute to the economic and social development of the communities where they operate and the world community at large), and slightly more specific stakeholder principles—essentially promises to obey the law and not to cheat. Human rights get a brief mention. But the Caux Principles' formulators point out one big selling point: because the document was devised by business leaders, its ethical norms are more likely than those from other sources to be

## Codes of Conduct Support Humane Treatment

As awareness of worker mistreatment has grown, foreign-owned firms—and, in particular, American-owned firms—have actively taken measures to ensure that workers are treated humanely. Companies have established codes of conduct for their suppliers. As the International Labor Organization reports, "Available information suggests that the world's largest multinational enterprises (MNEs), and in particular U.S.-based MNEs in the [textiles, clothing, footwear,] and related commerce sectors (e.g., manufacturers, retailers including department stores, mass merchandisers, specialty stores and mail order clothing companies), have led the trend toward usage of codes as a means of responsible sourcing."

*Aaron Lukas, "WTO Report Card III:*
*Globalization and Developing Countries," Cato Institute, 2000.*

broadly accepted by the business community. Many firms use the Caux Principles as the basis for their own codes of conduct.

These aspirational codes require no confirmation of whether firms are meeting their commitments. Because the codes are arising piecemeal—by the thousands, all with different specifications—comparing what various firms are promising to do is difficult. And many firms do no monitoring at all.

The second type of code is more demanding. It requires specific commitments on labor or environmental standards, along with independent confirmation of whether commitments are being met. Once a code is established, an independent external auditor comes in, assesses whether a company is in full compliance, and if so certifies it. The firm can then ad-

vertise its compliance and display the stamp of approval on its products. The nonprofit Council on Economic Priorities, in collaboration with human rights organizations, businesses, and auditing companies, devised a code of conduct called Social Accountability 8000, intended to become the global standard on workers' rights. Companies that adopt the code permit outside auditors to inspect every facility and assess practices on child labor, health and safety, freedom of association, the right to collective bargaining, discrimination, disciplinary practices, working hours, and—a matter excluded from most corporate codes—whether compensation provides workers a living wage.

Compliance with such externally monitored codes of conduct is completely voluntary. No government enforces them; no international organization has made the standards law. Instead, the assumption is that corporations will want to be so certified because they will find it good for business—because consumers will prefer to buy certified products.

How successful such codes will be remains unclear. A few big companies, including Toys R Us and Avon, have announced they will buy only from SA-8000-certified suppliers, and Avon is the first to be so certified. But some industry groups object strongly, arguing that the ever-mounting costs of certification with the growing array of standards are too great and that industry should set and monitor its own standards.

They have a point. Certification is expensive. Corporations are being flooded with demands to meet standard after standard. Some demands come from groups whose claim to represent a broad public interest seems dubious. It is not at all clear who should decide exactly what standards the codes should uphold.

## Who Will Watch the Watchers?

Another question is: "*Quis custodiet custodes*"—who will watch the watchers? The complexities show up in the current competition over who should monitor the treatment of overseas

labor by U.S. garment manufacturers, who are often accused of subjecting their workers to sweatshop conditions. On one side is the Fair Labor Association (FLA), the outcome of a Clinton administration presidential task force that included both human rights groups and major corporations. On the other is the Worker Rights Consortium (WRC), a university coalition formed by the United Students Against Sweatshops (USAS). The two groups hotly contest each other's motives, methods, and primary goals. FLA member companies agree to have conditions in their overseas contractors' factories monitored by independent agencies, but the company hires the monitor and the reports are not made public. The USAS says this is not good enough, and it set up the WRC to inspect factories that produce goods bearing the trademarks of and licensed by American colleges and universities.

Such problems are not surprising. The certification approach is essentially an effort to replace a government function—inspection—that even most governments have found difficult to do. There is no particular reason to think private inspectors will systematically do better than public ones or that private resources can readily be found to pay for necessary inspections if public resources are unavailable. By default, many of the private inspections are being carried out by big accounting firms, whose expertise lies in a different kind of inspection.

PricewaterhouseCoopers [PwC], the leader in "social accounting," allowed Dara O'Rourke, of the Massachusetts Institute of Technology, to accompany its auditors on factory inspections of labor practices in China and Korea. O'Rourke's report is disturbing. In one inspection, the PwC auditor found some questions she was supposed to ask workers "embarrassing" and skipped them; she answered other questions herself without bothering to ask the workers. In another, the factory president selected the workers to be interviewed, and the auditors skipped all questions about freedom of association, col-

lective bargaining, child labor, and forced labor, claiming that because the factory had no union the questions were not relevant. In both cases, the auditors, financial specialists who had gotten a crash course in social and environmental monitoring, missed major health and safety violations.

## The Global Compact

A third model can be found at the United Nations. In 1999, UN Secretary-General Kofi Annan promulgated a "Global Compact" which he asked corporations to sign to indicate voluntary adherence to nine widely accepted UN principles on human rights, labor standards, and the environment. Signatories are supposed to report annually on progress in implementing these principles. The Compact thus does not require outside certification but does insist on at least some degree of public accounting.

The Global Compact, like most compromises, provokes criticisms from both sides. Activist groups object to the unverified self-reporting, claiming that notorious corporate bad guys will be allowed to wrap themselves in the UN logo without making any real change. The head of the International Chamber of Commerce protests that "business should not be called upon to meet demands and expectations that are properly the preserve of governments."

Despite such skepticism, voluntary corporate codes may improve corporate behavior even without the coercion that backs up governmental regulation. Companies do care about their reputations. Reputations are increasingly going global, leaving corporations increasingly vulnerable to new pressures.

Even self-reporting systems such as the Global Compact could turn out to be more effective than expected if corporations take seriously (or are pressured into taking seriously) the reports they are supposed to file each year. Self-reporting, while not ideal, has two potentially beneficial effects. First, it forces the corporation to take a look at its own practices, if

only to justify them. Although many corporations will seize the opportunity to exercise the art of spin, some will discover things about themselves that they may want to change. Second, activist groups won't accept those reports at face value. Several groups have already promised to scrutinize them. By signing the Compact, the corporations have agreed to be held to standards of behavior going beyond what governmental regulations require. The activist groups intend to provide the fire to hold to the corporations' collective feet.

## Who Knows?

Whether the groups can do so depends on whether they can amass meaningful information about the degree of corporate compliance. The big missing piece in the corporate code puzzle has been how to make the necessary information public in some systematic fashion that makes it possible to compare organizations and to evaluate claims of good (or bad) behavior.

Into the morass has stepped the Global Reporting Initiative, a polyglot array of corporations, accounting firms, and environmental, human rights, and labor organizations, which has developed a framework for voluntary reporting on corporate economic, environmental, and social performance. Its Sustainability Reporting Guidelines, tested in draft form on 21 companies in the late 1990s, were revised in June 2000 and again in 2002. Already, companies are using the GRI framework to report on their compliance with the UN Global Compact.

## Who Cares?

All disclosure-based "regulation" depends on the assumption that someone somewhere cares about the information that gets released. The usual argument, especially by certifiers, is that consumers care, particularly consumers in rich countries with the buying power that impresses corporations. Unfortunately, the share of consumers who demonstrate a preference for "certified" goods is substantially lower than the share who

make that claim in marketing surveys. Consumer pressure has had far more success improving product safety than working conditions. It took unions—workers looking out for their own interests—to do that.

But corporations have other obligations besides those to consumers. They must also satisfy investors. And rapidly growing numbers of investors are adding social responsibility to their criteria for selecting companies in which to invest. Shareholder activism first became prominent in the late 1970s as part of an anti-apartheid campaign against South Africa and has flourished, most strikingly in the United States. In 1984, according to the Social Investment Forum, roughly $40 billion in U.S. assets under professional management had undergone some sort of social or environmental screening. By 1995, the total was $639 billion. Two years later, it had cracked the $1 trillion mark, and by 2001, it had reached $2.3 trillion.

What constitutes socially responsible behavior varies according to who is doing the screening. The single most widely used criterion is simple: no tobacco. Screens can include everything from environmental sustainability to treatment of workers to animal rights. Religious mutual funds and indexes use the beliefs of specific faiths as criteria.

Focusing on investors addresses one key legitimacy question about screening. Even in the most conservative perspective on the social role of the corporation, those who own it are entitled to a significant say in what goals it should be trying to achieve. And with evidence mounting that screened investments match or outperform the market, the $6 trillion locked up in U.S. pension funds may offer another avenue for growth. People who control workers' pensions just might find themselves under pressure to take seriously workers' rights.

## Regulation by Revelation

The effort to devise meaningful rules for global corporations matters greatly. Future global prosperity depends in part on whether corporate practices encourage a widespread sharing

of the benefits of economic integration, and future environmental stability depends on whether corporate activities are carried out in an environmentally sustainable fashion. The private sector could decide of its own volition to behave with the necessary degree of social responsibility, either out of altruism or from an enlightened view of long-term self-interest. Some will, but most probably will not. Nor will governments be able to regulate them into compliance with high standards, given the lack of capacity of many governments and the growing ability of corporations to pick up and leave any too-effective jurisdiction. Thus the need for credible regulation by revelation, using transparency to determine whether corporations are adhering to codes of socially responsible conduct.

Those who distrust corporations on principle will not be satisfied with such "soft law," and no one can yet be assured the approach will work on a large scale. This soft approach is an evolving process. Increasingly, corporations are being held to new standards of social responsibility that go far beyond legal requirements to enrich shareholders and obey the rules governments make. The dispute over exactly what those standards should be—and who should decide—has just begun.

> *"Since large auditing and consultancy firms usually carry out the monitoring of company codes with little transparency or public participation, whether the codes are actually being implemented or not remains a closely guarded secret. Besides, auditing firms may not reveal damaging information since they get paid by the company being audited."*

# Voluntary Codes of Conduct Will Not Make Corporations More Accountable

*Kavaljit Singh*

*Kavaljit Singh, the director of Public Interest Research Centre in New Delhi, India, and the author of* Why Investment Matters: The Political Economy of International Investments, *argues in this viewpoint that voluntary codes of conduct are tools that corporations use to manage their public reputations, and are not legally binding. Furthermore, he points out that many corporations with a low public profile do not adopt them. They do not impact a company's subcontractors, suppliers or franchisees, and*

Kavaljit Singh, "Corporate Accountability: Is Self Regulation the Answer?" Countercurrents.org, April 24, 2007. Reproduced by permission of the publisher and the author.

*are usually limited in scope to the most public aspects of a company's operations, Singh explains. For these and other reasons, Singh concludes that voluntary codes of conduct do not eliminate the need for regulation and enforcement by the nation states.*

As you read, consider the following questions:

1. Kavaljit Singh suggests that in the 1980s, countries like the United States encouraged the adoption of voluntary codes of conduct as an alternative to strict laws and regulations because it was assumed that transnational corporations would undertake social and environmental responsibilities voluntarily. Does he believe that this assumption was warranted?

2. What example does the author provide to support his view that voluntary codes of conduct usually set standards for corporate behavior that are less stringent than existing national laws?

3. According to this viewpoint, it is the responsibility of nation states to regulate the behavior of transnational corporations. To whom are nation states ultimately responsible?

The globalization of trade and investment flows has been paralleled by the emergence of Codes of Conduct. Although the first corporate code of conduct was created by the International Chamber of Commerce (ICC) in 1949, the 1990s witnessed a plethora of voluntary codes and corporate social responsibility (CSR) guidelines. There is no consensus on the precise definition of a code of conduct. Codes can range from one-page broad statements to detailed benchmarks and guidelines on how to conduct business practices globally. Voluntary approaches are based either on a self-regulation model or a co-regulation one between firms, citizen groups, and governments.

It is important to underscore that voluntary approaches did not emerge in a vacuum. Their emergence has more to do with a change in the paradigm of how global capital should be governed. Voluntary approaches, such as the Organization for International Cooperation and Development (OECD) Guidelines on Multinational Corporations, were a direct response to UN [United Nations] initiatives in the 1970s to regulate the activities of Transnational Corporations (TNCs). However, it needs to be emphasized that, unlike the UN initiatives, the OECD Guidelines were not aimed at protecting national sovereignty or addressing developmental concerns of the host countries, but at circumventing the UN initiatives.

The deregulation and 'free market' environment of the 1980s gave greater legitimacy to the self-regulation model embedded in the Anglo-Saxon business tradition. Many developed countries, particularly the US [United States], encouraged TNCs to adopt voluntary measures rather than enacting and enforcing strict laws governing their activities and behavior. The argument against regulation was based on the belief that TNCs would undertake greater social and environmental responsibilities through voluntary measures.

## Voluntary Initiatives Protect Reputations

In the late 1980s, campaigns launched by NGOs [nongovernmental organizations] and consumer groups brought significant changes in the public perception of corporate behavior, which in turn facilitated the further proliferation of voluntary initiatives. Campaigns in the developed countries focusing on popular consumer brands such as Nike and Levi's brought to public notice some of the appalling working and environmental conditions in some of these companies' overseas production sites. Realizing that bad publicity could seriously damage corporate and brand reputations and that their products could face consumer boycotts, many corporations suddenly started adopting codes of conduct and other CSR

measures. Since the early 1990s, the majority of voluntary measures have been undertaken by individual corporations. US-based corporations were the first to introduce codes of conduct with jeans manufacturer Levi's adopting one in 1992.

Pressures generated by the 'ethical' investor community and other shareholders also contributed to the proliferation of voluntary measures.

Given that there is often a considerable discrepancy between a corporation undertaking to follow a voluntary code and its actual business conduct (e.g., Nike), many critics argue that CSR measures have become corporate public relations tools used to create a positive corporate image. In today's competitive world, a positive image as a responsible company adds significant value to a company's business and reputation and helps it manage various risks. Thus, the growing popularity of voluntary measures in recent years has not ended debates on how to regulate TNC corporate behavior. . . .

## The Limits of Voluntary Approaches

Voluntary approaches have several inherent weaknesses and operational difficulties. . . . Corporate codes are purely voluntary, non-binding instruments. No corporation can be held legally accountable for violating them. The responsibility to implement the code rests entirely on the corporation. At best, corporations can be forced to implement codes only through moral persuasion and public pressure.

Second, despite being in existence for many years, the number of companies adopting such codes is still relatively small. Moreover, corporate codes are limited to a few sectors, particularly those in which brand names are important in corporate sales, such as garments, footwear, consumer goods, and retailing businesses. A large number of other sectors remain outside the purview of corporate codes.

Third, many codes are still not universally binding on all the operations of a company, including its contractors, subsid-

iaries, suppliers, agents, and franchisees. Codes rarely encompass the workers in the informal sector, who could well be an important part of a company's supply chain. Further, a company may implement only one type of code, for instance, an environmental one, while neglecting other important codes related to labor protection, and health and safety.

Fourth, corporate codes are limited in scope and often set standards that are lower than existing national regulations. For instance, labor codes recognize the right to freedom of association but do not provide the right to strike. In many countries, such as India, the right to strike is a legally recognized instrument.

Fifth, the mushrooming of voluntary codes in an era of deregulated business raises serious doubts about their efficacy. There is an increasing concern that corporate codes are being misused to deflect public criticism of corporate activities and to reduce the demand for state regulation of corporations. In some cases, codes have actually worsened working conditions and the bargaining power of labor unions. Moreover, increasing numbers of NGO-business partnerships established through corporate codes and CSR measures have created and widened divisions within the NGO community and sharpened differences between NGOs and labor unions. Voluntary codes of conduct can never substitute for state regulations. Nor can they substitute for labor and community rights. At best, voluntary codes can complement state regulations and provide an opportunity to raise environmental, health, labor, and other public interest issues.

## Implementation Can Be a Challenge

Despite the recent proliferation of codes, their actual implementation and monitoring remain problematic. Information about codes is generally not available to workers and consumers. Researchers have found that labor codes have often been introduced in companies without the prior knowledge or con-

sent of the workers for whom they are intended. A key issue regarding the implementation process is the independence of the monitoring body. Since large auditing and consultancy firms usually carry out the monitoring of company codes with little transparency or public participation, whether the codes are actually being implemented or not remains a closely guarded secret. Besides, auditing firms may not reveal damaging information since they get paid by the company being audited.

Recent voluntary initiatives, such as Multi-Stakeholder Initiatives (MSIs), are considered more credible because NGOs and labor unions are involved as external monitors. But the authenticity of such monitoring cannot be guaranteed by the mere involvement of NGOs and civil society.

Researchers have found that the development of standards by some MSIs has taken place in a top-down manner without the involvement of workers at the grassroots level. For instance, concerns of workers in India and Bangladesh were not taken into account in the standards created by MSIs such as the Ethical Trading Initiative and Social Accountability International. If recent experience is any guide, the struggle to implement codes could be frustrating, time-consuming, and ultimately futile. It dissipates any enthusiasm to struggle for regulatory controls on TNCs. This was evident in the case of the decade-long campaign in India on a national code to promote breast-feeding and restrict the marketing of baby food by TNCs along the lines of WHO [World Health Organization] code. Therefore, voluntary codes require serious rethinking on the part of those who consider them as a cure-all to problems posed by TNCs.

The unveiling of corporate scandals (from Worldcom to Enron to Parmalat) underline the important role of strong regulatory measures. One cannot ignore the fact that all these corporations were signatories to several international codes while some of them (for instance, Enron) had developed their own codes.

## Why State Regulation?

The proponents of neoliberal ideology argue that states should abdicate their legislative and enforcement responsibilities by handing them over to NGOs and civil society organizations which should develop voluntary measures in collaboration with business. Without undermining the relevance of such voluntary approaches, it cannot be denied that the primary responsibility of regulating corporate behavior of TNCs remains with nation states. It is difficult to envisage the regulation of TNCs without the active involvement of states. State regulations are the primary vehicle for local and national government and international institutions to implement public policies. National governments have the primary responsibility of protecting and improving the social and economic conditions of all citizens, particularly the poorer and more vulnerable ones.

There is no denying that all states are not democratic and that supervisory mechanisms are often weak, particularly in developing countries. Despite these shortcomings, however, states remain formally accountable to their citizens, whereas corporations are accountable only to their shareholders. National regulatory measures are also necessary to implement international frameworks. The additional advantage of national regulatory measures is that they would be applicable to all companies, domestic or transnational, operating under a country's jurisdiction, thereby maximizing welfare gains.

The national regulatory framework is very important and it will not wither away under the influence of globalization. On its own, transnational capital lacks the necessary power and ability to mould the world economy in its favor. Rather, it strives for the support of nation-states and inter-state institutions to shape the contemporary world economy. State policies are vital for the advancement and sustenance of transnational capital on a world scale. Investment decisions by TNCs are not always influenced by the degree of national liberaliza-

# The Profitable Logic of Cheap Labor

"Sweatshops are absolutely not limited to apparel," says Charles Kernaghan of the National Labor Committee in New York City. "Sporting goods, electronics, shoes, sneakers, agricultural products, coffee, bananas—you name it—it's made under some pretty rough conditions—in factories in Malaysia, the Philippines, Indonesia." . . .

In 1996, public concerns about overseas sweatshops prompted congressional hearings, lofty promises by apparel companies to more closely monitor their contractors and a presidential task force on the issue. In April 1997, following leafleting by the US/Guatemala Labor Education Campaign, Starbucks Coffee finally took action towards a pilot project that will implement a more humane code of conduct by coffee growers toward workers in Guatemala.

But so far there's no sign of a wide-spread shift toward restraints on child labor, better pay or safer working conditions. One reason for this is that new international trade pacts, such as GATT [General Agreement on Tariffs and Trade] and NAFTA [North American Free Trade Agreement], make it difficult to enact sanctions against countries that permit labor abuses. And another reason is the obvious one: these cheap labor pools are enormously profitable for American corporations.

*Jeffrey St. Clair, Born Under a Bad Sky.*
*Oakland, CA: AK Press. 2008.*

tion but are also governed by state regulations in areas as diverse as taxation, trade, investment, currency, property rights, and labor.

## The Benefits of Regulation

A stable economic and political environment is also an important determinant. Transnational capital looks upon legislative, judicial, and executive institutions not merely to protect and enforce property rights and contract laws, but also to provide social, political, and macroeconomic stability. In the absence of such a policy framework, contemporary globalization would not have taken place. Social and political conflicts are also resolved primarily through state mechanisms. The fact that a strong and stable state is a prerequisite for the development and sustenance of the market economy is evident from the failure of economic reforms in transition countries. In addition, state intervention is also necessary to prevent and correct market failures. There are innumerable instances of market failures with huge economic, social, and environmental costs throughout the world. Pollution and monopoly power are the most popular examples of market failure. The government can introduce pollution taxes and regulate monopolies to correct the distortions created by market failure. Besides, the government is expected to provide public goods and services (for example, schools, hospitals, and highways) to all citizens because the market has failed to do so.

In the context of global capitalism, nation-states provide the legal framework within which all markets operate. The notion of a 'free market' is a myth because all markets are governed by regulations, though the nature and degree of regulation may vary from market to market. Even the much-claimed self-regulation or co-regulation model would lack legitimacy if it was not backed by a government decree. In fact, it is impossible to conceive of contemporary neoliberal globalization without laws, which do not exist outside the realm of

nation-states. Even the global rules on trade enforced by international institutions (for instance, WTO) are not independent of nation-states.

## What Should Be Regulated?

The first step towards regulating TNC behavior begins at the national level. Host countries in particular should adopt appropriate regulatory measures on transparency, labor, environmental, and taxation matters. At the same time, home countries should put in place regulations to ensure that the same standards are followed by their TNCs irrespective of where they operate in the world. The Foreign Corrupt Practices Act of the US, which penalizes US-based corporations for their bribery and corrupt practices in foreign countries, is a case in point.

National regulatory measures could be supplemented by new forms of regulatory cooperation and coordination between states at regional and international levels. By providing the overall framework and guiding principles, regional and international efforts should enhance the policy space and powers to regulate TNCs and foreign investment in order to meet national developmental objectives.

At the domestic level, the political climate in many developing countries has drastically changed in the past two decades. Neoliberal policies now frame almost every political process and go unchallenged even among some ranks of the left. There is a strong lobby in many developing countries (for instance, India) consisting of big business, the upper middle classes and the media, which supports the entry of foreign capital and demands fewer regulatory mechanisms. Some developing countries like India and China are also witnessing the emergence of 'Third world TNCs' that are expanding their businesses in other countries. These developments make the task of regulating corporations still more difficult. How can such countries demand greater regulation of private capital

flows? Besides, it fragments the coalitions of developing countries and weakens their collective bargaining power in international economic policy arenas such as the WTO. Nonetheless, even though the task of re-establishing the authority of states over TNCs may be difficult, it would not be impossible provided efforts were backed by strong domestic political mobilization. Herein the role of NGOs, labor unions, and other civil society organizations becomes important to strengthen domestic political processes.

## Strong Supervision Is a Requirement

It needs to be stressed here that a robust, transparent and efficient supervisory framework is also required to oversee the implementation of national regulations. Otherwise expected gains from a strong regulatory framework would not materialize. India provides a classic example of having a strong regulatory framework but poor supervisory structures. In the present world, there is a need for greater international supervision of private investment flows based on cooperation between home country and host country supervisors.

While acknowledging that voluntary approaches could be used as tools for leverage on corporate behavior and therefore are worth testing, this . . . underscores the need for enhancing the state regulatory and supervisory frameworks. Any strategy aimed at privatizing regulation is bound to fail; even the limited gains made in the past through voluntary approaches always rested on governmental backing. Voluntary codes of conduct can never be a substitute for state regulations. Nor can they substitute for labor and community rights. At best, voluntary codes can complement state regulations and provide space for raising environmental, health, labor, and other public interest issues. As rightly pointed out by Rhys Jenkins, "Codes of conduct should be seen as an area of political contestation, rather than as a solution to the problems created by the globalization of economic activity."

> "Many people and groups are 'sceptics',
> regarding corporate responsibility as
> old-fashioned public relations (PR)
> with the aim of distracting society from
> the need for more effective regulation
> of corporate activity and transforma-
> tion to an economic system grounded
> in the ecological and social realities of
> the planet."

# Some Nongovernmental Organizations Are Challenging the Rhetoric of the Corporate Social Responsibility Movement

*Jem Bendell*

*Jem Bendell, a researcher, consultant, educator, and writer, has published two books on corporate social responsibility. In this viewpoint, he argues that many nongovernmental organizations (NGOs) that once were supporters of the corporate social responsibility (CSR) movement have become disenchanted, and now believe that CSR is nothing more than a way of diverting attention from the need for effective laws and regulations. Rather*

Jem Bendell, "Heading for Divorce," *Lifeworth*, Winter 2004. Reproduced by permission.

*than becoming defensive, he says, corporate social responsibility leaders should engage the dialogue and reflect on their practice. Bendell contends, that those leaders should respond seriously to valid criticisms while continuing to articulate the strong case for CSR and its benefits to society.*

As you read, consider the following questions:

1. What is the first evidence the author presents that some nongovernmental organizations have lost their enthusiasm for the corporate social responsibility movement?

2. What was it about the Christian Aid report, *Behind the Mask*, that drew the criticism of Mallen Baker? Does the author feel this is a valid criticism?

3. The author of this viewpoint employs the image of a marriage to model the relationship between corporate CSR officials and nongovernmental organizations. What point is he trying to make about the future of corporate social responsibility?

So the honeymoon is over. After a decade of increasingly closer relations between business and NGOs [nongovernmental organizations], which contributed to the birth of a revitalised concept or corporate social responsibility (CSR), the strains are beginning to show. In the UK [United Kingdom], which is seen by many to have been at the forefront of this area, many NGOs are now turning their backs on CSR initiatives, or even making them the focus of criticism and campaigns. For example, international development groups like the World Development Movement, Action Aid, New Economics Foundation, War on Want and Christian Aid are not as active in the Ethical Trading Initiative (ETI), which they all helped to found and which brought them together with companies to work on improving labour conditions in corporate supply chains.

"Key NGOs have now turned their back on the opportunity that [corporate citizenship] represents, to fall back on

easy anti-corporate messages that play well to their core constituencies," said Mallen Baker, of Business in the Community, in February [2004]. He was commenting after the British charity Christian Aid, had made criticism of CSR initiatives the mainstay of its campaign to push for global regulations for global corporations. "The image of multinational companies working hard to make the world a better place is often just that—'an image" said Christian Aid's report *Behind the Mask*, published in January [2004] "What's needed are new laws to make businesses responsible for protecting human rights and the environment wherever they work," they said, and that CSR initiatives are used by many companies to undermine progress towards such laws. That some people involved in, or commenting on, initiatives that might be labelled CSR, sometimes use their existence to push a neo-liberal economic agenda was identified as a key challenge in previous reviews, as was the need to see corporate support for, or lobbying against, mandatory mechanisms for improved social and environmental conduct as a key dimension to a company's social responsibility.

## Evaluating Case Studies

Some criticised Christian Aid's report for not engaging with the companies it was attacking or not conducting a more systemic analysis of the impacts of CSR. For example, Mallen Baker suggested that as the report featured just three case studies, even if everything Christian Aid said about those were true, it wouldn't mean that the wider CSR or corporate citizenship community discourse and practice is defunct. However, Christian Aid is not the only one whose methodology can be criticised. Much academic management research employs case studies to build concepts, arguments, and theories, while think tanks, corporations, and consulting firms often use case studies as the basis for positive assessments of the potential and reality of corporate social responsibility and cor-

## Views on Corporate Social Responsibility (CSR)

Critics: Anti-CSR [corporate social responsibility], seeing it as distracting business from securing profits. Some are market fundamentalists, believing the pursuit of self-interest will create the greatest social gain. Others see that government has a role to play and CSR can distract us from this.

Evangelicals: Pro-CSR, believing there is a win-win relationship between business and society, and that everyone can do well by doing good. The fact there are still problems is a result of people not realising the benefits of CSR.

Pragmatics: Pro-CSR, believing that there are some win-wins between business and society but that there are also situations where business needs to be regulated, or rewarded, to ensure socially acceptable performance.

Ambivalents: Neither pro- nor anti-CSR, regarding that it could be beneficial for some aspects of society and some business's but that it involves the intrusion of commercial values into the realms of the social and human, so it is worrying.

Sceptics: Anti-CSR, believing that it is largely a public relations exercise to further empower business to control the lives of people in the pursuit of profit maximisation, and distracts our attention from the need to regulate corporate power.

*Jem Bendell, "Heading for Divorce,"*
Lifeworth, *Winter 2004. Reproduced by permission.*

porate citizenship. The use of case studies must be tempered with the knowledge of their particularity, partialness and, pos-

sibly, partiality. Case studies are useful for allowing a richness and depth of understanding, and for their powers of explanation or evocation. However, it's difficult to generalise from a sample of one, or even three. Therefore quantitative studies may add another dimension to our understanding of the nature of corporate responsibility. One person who attempted such work is Professor Richard Marens of California State University. He suggests that if corporations in the United States have indeed been tending to the interests of their diverse stakeholders, especially over the past 20 years since Ed Freeman published his articulation of the stakeholder concept of management, then it should be reflected in key statistics. However, he notes that nation-wide statistics show average wages have declined and working hours increased in America, while employee security and benefits have declined. Considering tax-payers to be a key stakeholder, he notes how corporate taxes have fallen and more public funds been spent on private corporations. In addition to these indicators of corporate impacts on society, we could consider pollution levels. Carbon emissions in the United States have increased by over 15% since 1990—globally carbon emissions have increased over 10% in the past decade. The release of toxic chemicals has fallen, but this can be attributed to the Emergency Planning and Community Right to Know Act of 1986 (which requires companies to register information on their use, storage and release of toxic substances), rather than a voluntary responsibility effort alone. These statistics suggest that if we leave aside case studies, there is little evidence to suggest that those practices we label CSR or corporate citizenship are having a significant effect on the big picture—as yet.

## Many Are Sceptical—but Defensiveness Will Not Help

Christian Aid's criticism of CSR is not unique or novel. Many people and groups are "sceptics", regarding corporate respon-

sibility as old-fashioned public relations (PR) with the aim of distracting society from the need for more effective regulation of corporate activity and transformation to an economic system grounded in the ecological and social realities of the planet. On the other side of the political spectrum there are the critics of corporate responsibility who see it as distracting business managers from securing profits for the owners of corporations. "From an ethical point of view, the problem with conscientious CSR (as opposed to fake) CSR is obvious: it is philanthropy at other people's expense" said *The Economist*, in an article commenting on the Christian Aid report. Between these negative poles there are people who are fairly evangelical, pragmatic or ambivalent about CSR.

To be defensive when criticised is an understandable reaction. However, our hope is we might see more corporate responsibility professionals engaging with critics and sceptics. The critics make it more important for us to be clear on what we believe to be the business case for corporate responsibility. The sceptics make it more important for us to be clear on what we believe to be the people's case for corporate responsibility—in other words, the benefit for society. We need critics and sceptics to help us reflect on our own practice, assumptions and interests, and ensure we are authentic in what we do.

We have come a long way since the mid-1990s when business and NGOs were thought to be risking *Sleeping With the Enemy* by working with each other, and the turn of the millennium when they were said to be *Getting Engaged* and then enjoying a "honeymoon period for corporate responsibility". The word honeymoon comes from the tradition of a married couple drinking fermented honey for a month after their marriage. Might business and NGOs be realizing they've been drunk on the hope and novelty of their initial engagement? Could this sobering up lead to a permanent divorce, with fights in the courts of law and public opinion?

As we suggest above, we hope that conflict will not be the only outcome, but that it might lead to a transformation of the relationship between business and society, and perhaps even a new level of collaboration and dialogue that focuses on how to drive systemic changes in the global political economy.

*"Not only do businesses have a responsibility to behave ethically, but virtue itself can pay."*

# Business Schools Should Integrate Social Responsibility Across the Curriculum

*Elizabeth Armstrong*

*In the following viewpoint, Elizabeth Armstrong, who is a staff writer at* The Christian Science Monitor, *argues that businesses can be socially responsible while also making money. Business schools, at places such as Brandeis University, are teaching this message in corporate social responsibility courses. Corporate social responsibility first came to light in the 1970s in the wake of Watergate and other business scandals. However, it took the recent Enron and WorldCom scandals to get more than a handful of schools to include the concept in their curriculums.*

As you read, consider the following questions:

1. How long has corporate social responsibility been a part of business school curriculums?
2. What is the "triple bottom line"?

Elizabeth Armstrong, "The Value of Virtue," *The Christian Science Monitor*, March 4, 2003. Reproduced by permission from Christian Science Monitor, (www.csmonitor.com).

181

3. In a recent AACSB survey of business schools, what percentage integrates corporate social responsibility into their core curriculum?

When Gail Snowden talks about making profit off the "disadvantaged" in "poor neighborhoods," like Harlem in New York and Roxbury in Boston, not a single person in the classroom flinches.

Most of these 40 graduate students at Brandeis University [Waltham, MA] are in business school precisely because they want to learn how to make money. And today, their pencils are flying.

But Ms. Snowden, president of the FleetBoston Financial Foundation in Boston, isn't discussing profit alone. A black woman raised in a family of social activists, Snowden spent years convincing corporate higher-ups that underserved communities would prove a vibrant resource for Fleet. Today she heads Fleet's Community Investment Group, which directs resources into low—and moderate—income communities.

Her work is just one proof, she says, that corporations can make money by being socially responsible.

## A More Prominent Place for CSR

This reinforces the two-fold message of Prof. Michael Appell's new course, "Corporations and Communications": Not only do businesses have a responsibility to behave ethically, but virtue itself can pay.

"We focus on the subject of return on responsibility," Mr. Appell says. "Overall, companies that take CSR [corporate social responsibility] seriously outperform those that do not."

The concept of CSR has been a part of some business school curriculums since the 1970s, but it has earned a more prominent place in the wake of recent business scandals. CSR is distinct, however, from business ethics, an older term that deals with misbehavior, such as fraud, within a company. CSR

examines the impact a corporation has on the world around it—by, say, reviving an abandoned neighborhood or improving the working conditions of its factories in a developing country.

"I want my students to set aside whatever assumptions they have about NGOs [nongovernmental organizations] and business," Appell says—specifically, the notion that NGOs do good work while businesses make money, and that the two are mutually exclusive.

The students' own backgrounds help to challenge that dichotomy. They come from a dozen countries and two very different graduate programs—one focused on business and another on international development.

Deanna Becker, a student in the Heller School for Social Policy and Management and one of the few Americans in the class, is taking the course to learn more about the way businesses operate.

"I'm in the sustainable international development program, and we talk about all sorts of paths toward development," she says.

"But one of the things that often gets left out is that there's the force of business out there. I wanted to be in a class that actually addresses the impact that businesses have."

## Decades in the Making

"Business ethics" has long been considered an oxymoron. In 1906, historian Ambrose Bierce defined the corporation as "an ingenious device for obtaining profit without individual responsibility."

In 1970, soon after the term "corporate social responsibility" was coined, economist Milton Friedman echoed Bierce's sentiments in the *New York Times*: "There is one and only one responsibility of business—to use its resources and engage in activities designed to increase its profits."

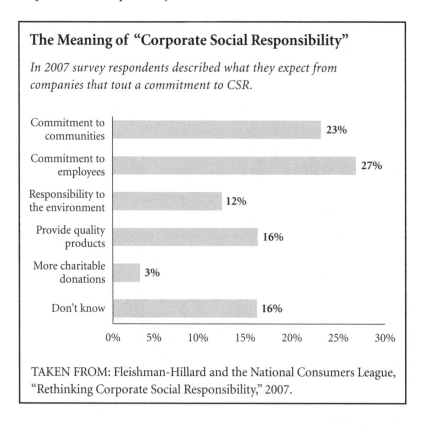

**The Meaning of "Corporate Social Responsibility"**

*In 2007 survey respondents described what they expect from companies that tout a commitment to CSR.*

Commitment to communities — 23%

Commitment to employees — 27%

Responsibility to the environment — 12%

Provide quality products — 16%

More charitable donations — 3%

Don't know — 16%

0%  5%  10%  15%  20%  25%  30%

TAKEN FROM: Fleishman-Hillard and the National Consumers League, "Rethinking Corporate Social Responsibility," 2007.

But in the mid-1970s, with the Watergate brouhaha still echoing and a string of business scandals revealing massive fraudulence and waste, the mere discussion of ethics was deemed insufficient. Whistle blowers turned to professors for help in the hopes that academia might influence a new generation of business leaders.

A handful of schools began to teach the "triple bottom line"—the idea that corporations should focus not just on economics, but on their social and environmental values as well. But these classes were few and far between.

Academic philosophers who taught business ethics, many of whom were also employed by corporations as morality consultants, began to argue that CSR needed to be included in the discussion. But it wasn't until the end of 2001, when Enron and WorldCom executives were caught with their fists in

the cookie jar, that classes began to look at the value of incorporating CSR into ethics courses.

"Many schools have increased or strengthened their corporate social responsibility and ethics coverage in required courses," says Daniel LeClair of the Association to Advance Collegiate Schools of Business International (AACSB) in St. Louis.

AACSB recently surveyed 119 business schools in the US [United States] and found that almost 90 percent integrate CSR into the core curriculum. About 30 percent also offer a stand-alone course akin to Appell's.

## A Variety of Speakers

But his class structure may be unique: "I wanted to bring in speakers from a variety of different settings who could tell the class what it's like on the ground in this world of social responsibility," he says.

Early in the semester, Charlie Rogers, manager of vendor compliance for Hasbro Inc., discussed improvements the company made in the living conditions of its factory workers in Asia. In turn, he said, the business had become more efficient—and more profitable.

Thomas Siekman, former general counsel and head of the ethics committee at Compaq, spoke about the importance of honest corporate behavior, and how it is key to instilling trust in its customers.

Steve Waddell, founder of Global Action Networks/Net, was invited to explain the Global Reporting Initiative, an attempt to develop international standards of ethics and conduct for businesses.

"There are some very important decisions out there that people need to make," says Marty Taylor, vice president of organizational services at the Institute for Global Ethics in Camden, Maine.

"Our work with kids indicates that the first step is creating awareness [about responsibility]," he says. "And the second step is figuring out how to do it."

Which is why Appell invites so many speakers to his class. "I want them to meet the actual people who are making a difference, so that we can talk about the role of leadership and understand what motivates them—and how they have been able to be a force for change within a variety of different bureaucracies," says Appell, himself a former president of one of the world's largest industry-sponsored charitable organizations, Two/Ten International Footwear Foundation.

## "Ripple Effects"

One course on corporate responsibility is not enough, says W. Michael Hoffman, executive director at Bentley College's Center for Business Ethics, also in Waltham.

"When I grade my students on grammar, I'll get this comment . . . that they'd already passed that course. We ought not to let that happen to ethics. They have to feel it's an integral part of being business leaders."

Appell agrees. "This is a beginning—and a good one—but only a beginning." Yet he remains optimistic that "there's a ripple effect that comes out of a course like this, where students get excited, talk to their peers, and bring these concepts into their careers. With the right information and motivation, they can become successful in the business and social sector and can make an enormous difference."

# Periodical Bibliography

*The following articles have been selected to supplement the diverse views presented in this chapter.*

Carlye Adler                "Can Corporations Save the World?" *Forbes*, November 28, 2006.

Betsy Atkins                "Is Corporate Social Responsibility Responsible?" *Forbes*, November 28, 2006.

Barnaby J. Feder            "Group Sets Corporate Code on Environmental Conduct," *New York Times*, September 8, 2008.

Thomas Hoffman              "Online Reputation Management: Cleaning Up Your Image Is Hot, But Is It Ethical?" *Computerworld*, March 17, 2008.

Richard Lambert             "The Path Back to Trust, Truth and Integrity," *The Guardian*, January 17, 2005.

Jim Lobe                    "Church Groups Launch Global Corporate Code of Conduct," Inter Press Service News Agency, May 20, 2008.

*Marketing Week*            "Reputation Management Is Now Key to a Brand's Success," September 25, 2008.

Ken Moore                   "Human Resources & Corporate Social Responsibility," *The Employment Times*, August 16, 2007.

*PR Weekly*                 "Campaign: Is CSR Doing Anything for Corporate Reputations?" January 18, 2008.

John Tozzi                  "Do Reputation Management Services Work? A New Industry Promises to Help Counter Negative Search Results on the Web," *Business Week Online*, May 1, 2008. www.businessweek.com.

# For Further Discussion

## Chapter 1

1. When Milton Friedman wrote his article, "The Social Responsibility of Business Is to Increase Its Profits," in 1970, it quickly became a classic. In recent years, however, stakeholder theory as explained by John Mackey in the first viewpoint has become much more widely accepted as an alternative perspective. What events can you think of that may have influenced broader acceptance of the view that businesses are responsible not only to their investors, but also to workers, customers and the communities where they are located?

2. Corporate social responsibility advocates assert that business should assume a major role in making the world a better place. Can you think of any reasons why businesses, in particular, should be expected to do this?

3. Do you agree with James K. Glassman that the corporate social responsibility movement represents a departure from free market capitalism, or do you think it is more of a developmental trend within free market capitalism?

4. What are some of the ways that globalization has contributed to the development of the corporate social responsibility movement?

## Chapter 2

1. Nick Schultz claims that as countries become wealthier, they also become greener and cleaner. Do you agree? Why or why not?

2. What are some of the reasons why John Lorinc says it does "pay to be green"? Do you think the argument that

there are cost savings to be realized in adopting more efficient energy technologies will be persuasive in the long run?

3. Tim Osborn-Jones argues that personal change must precede organizational change, and he puts a lot of faith in the possibility of personal transformation. Do you think the kind of transformation Osborn-Jones talks about is possible, and that it can make a significant difference in corporations' environmental conduct?

4. Companies that attempt to create a cleaner environmental profile frequently end up being accused of greenwashing. Can you think of any circumstances where these kinds of accusations might be unfair? Is there a way to distinguish greenwash from legitimate efforts to adopt environmentally sound business practices?

## Chapter 3

1. What are some of the ways globalization has made it easier for corporations to commit human rights abuses and get away with it?

2. In a world where so many corporations have become multinational in scope, what is the best way to ensure that human rights abuses do not occur?

3. What role, if any, do you think the United Nations should play in preventing human rights abuses?

4. What responsibility do national governments have to prevent human rights abuses?

## Chapter 4

1. Do you think it is possible to regulate the conduct of multinational corporations?

2. What do you think is the most effective approach to achieving greater corporate accountability for the environment and greater respect for human rights in the international business community?

# Organizations to Contact

*The editors have compiled the following list of organizations concerned with the issues debated in this book. The descriptions are derived from materials provided by the organizations. All have publications or information available for interested readers. The list was compiled on the date of publication of the present volume; the information provided here may change. Be aware that many organizations take several weeks or longer to respond to inquiries, so allow as much time as possible.*

## The Brookings Institution
1775 Massachusetts Avenue NW, Washington, DC   20036
(202) 797-6000
Web site: www.brookings.edu

The Brookings Institution, a nonprofit public policy organization based in Washington, D.C., conducts research and develops policy recommendations in support of a strong democracy, economic and social welfare, and a prosperous international economy. Brookings Institution research interests include economics, the global economy and development.

## Business for Social Responsibility (BSR)
111 Sutter Street, 12th Floor, San Francisco, CA   94104
(415) 984-3200 • Fax: (415) 984-3201
E-mail: Web@bsr.org
Web site: www.bsr.org

Business for Social Responsibility (BSR) is a nonprofit business association. Through consulting services, conferences and research, BSR works with corporations and concerned stakeholders of all types to create a more just and sustainable global economy. The BSR Web site provides a variety of resources on sustainable development in the global economy, and offers an archive of news articles on recent corporate social responsibility initiatives.

## Competitive Enterprise Institute
1001 Connecticut Avenue NW, Washington, DC   20036
(202) 331-1010 • Fax: (202) 331-0640
E-mail: info@cei.org
Web site: http://cei.org

The Competitive Enterprise Institute is a nonprofit public policy organization for the advancement of principles of free enterprise and limited government. Its Web site publishes articles and opinion pieces, as well as research, on a wide range of subjects including consumer protection, food safety, environmental risk management, and alternative energy.

## Human Rights Watch
350 Fifth Avenue, 34th Floor, New York, NY   10118-3299
(212) 290-4700 • Fax: (212) 736-1300
E-mail: hrwnyc@hrw.org
Web site: http://hrw.org

Human Rights Watch, an independent, nongovernmental organization, works to enlist the public and the international community to support the cause of human rights. It conducts fact-finding investigations into alleged violations, publishes its findings, and challenges governments and the business community to adopt policies and practices that respect human rights. Corporations, economic, social and cultural rights, and the rights of workers are among the issues addressed on the Human Rights Watch Web site.

## International Business Ethics Institute (IBEI)
1776 I Street NW, 9th Floor, Washington, DC   20006
(202) 296-6938 • Fax: (202) 296-5897
E-mail: info@business-ethics.org
Web site: www.business-ethics.org

The International Business Ethics Institute (IBEI) promotes business ethics and corporate responsibility by working to increase public awareness and dialogue about international business ethics. It also works closely with companies to assist them in establishing effective international ethics programs.

## Natural Resources Defense Council (NRDC)
40 West Twentieth Street, New York, NY   10011
(212) 727-2700 • Fax: (212) 727-1773
E-mail: nrdcinfo@nrdc.org
Web site: www.nrdc.org

Natural Resources Defense Council (NRDC) is a membership organization committed to environmental action. NRDC works to solve problems like global warming and chemical pollution, to advocate for clean energy technologies, and to protect the oceans and the natural environment. The NRDC Web site includes extensive resources designed to assist corporations with the task of developing environmentally responsible business practices.

## Realizing Rights
271 Madison Avenue, Suite 1007, New York, NY   10016
(212) 895-8080
E-mail: info@eginitiative.org
Web site: www.realizingrights.org

Realizing Rights was founded in 2002 by Mary Robinson, former President of Ireland, and former United Nations High Commissioner for Human Rights. The mission of Realizing Rights is to highlight the importance of human rights in the era of globalization and to assure that the needs of the most vulnerable, in areas such as health care, international trade and development and immigration, are addressed in a responsible way. Realizing Rights facilitates relationships between decision makers and key stakeholders, develops policy recommendations, and advocates for just laws and governance practices in the international arena.

## The World Bank
1818 H Street NW, Washington, DC   20433
(202) 473-1000 • Fax: (202) 477-6391
Web site: www.worldbank.org

The mission of The World Bank is to help developing countries and their people reach the Millennium Development Goals, adopted by the United Nations, by working with their

partners in government and industry to alleviate poverty. It seeks to build a strong investment climate to support jobs and sustainable growth. The World Bank Web site includes resources that address issues such as its development priorities, climate and clean energy, and the social and environmental footprint of The World Bank.

**World Business Council for Sustainable Development (WBCSD)**
1744 R Street NW, Washington, DC    20009
(202) 420-7745 • Fax: (202) 265-1662
E-mail: info@wbcsd.org
Web site: www.wbcsd.org

The World Business Council for Sustainable Development (WBCSD) is a global association of company CEOs concerned with business and sustainable development. The Council provides a platform for companies to explore sustainable development, share knowledge, experiences and best practices, and to advocate business positions on these issues in a variety of forums, working with governments, and nongovernmental and intergovernmental organizations.

# Bibliography of Books

Patricia Aburdene    *Megatrends 2010: The Rise of Conscious Capitalism.* Charlottesville, VA: Hampton Roads Publishing Company, 2005.

David Ahrens    *Investing in Vice: The Recession-Proof Portfolio of Booze, Bets, Bombs, and Butts.* New York: St. Martin's Press, 2004.

Mark Albion    *True to Yourself: Leading a Values-Based Business.* San Francisco, CA: Berrett-Koehler Publishers, Inc., 2006.

Christine Arena    *The High Purpose Company.* New York: HarperCollins, 2007.

David Batstone    *Saving the Corporate Soul & (Who Knows?) Maybe Your Own.* San Francisco, CA: Jossey Bass, 2003.

Sharon Beder    *Global Spin: The Corporate Assault on Environmentalism.* White River Junction, VT: Chelsea Green Publishing Company, 2002.

Stephen M.R. Covey    *The Speed of Trust: The One Thing That Changes Everything.* New York: Free Press, 2006.

Howard Gardner    *Responsibility at Work: How Leading Professionals Act (or Don't Act) Responsibly.* San Francisco, CA: Jossey-Bass, 2007.

John C.
Harrington

*The Challenge to Power: Money, Investing and Democracy.* White River Junction, VT: Chelsea Green Publishing Company, 2005.

Hazel Henderson

*Ethical Markets: Growing the Green Economy.* White River Junction, VT: Chelsea Green Publishing Company, 2006.

Gary Hirshberg

*Stirring It Up: How to Make Money and Save the World.* New York: Hyperion, 2008.

Jeffrey Hollender

*What Matters Most: How a Small Group of Pioneers Is Teaching Social Responsibility to Big Business, and Why Big Business Is Listening.* New York: Basic Books, 2004.

John Kasich

*Stand for Something: The Battle for America's Soul.* New York: Warner Books, 2006.

Christine C.
MacDonald

*Green, Inc.: An Environmental Insider Reveals How a Good Cause Has Gone Bad.* Guilford, CT: Lyons Press, 2008.

Lynn Sharp Paine

*Value Shift: Why Companies Must Merge Social and Financial Imperatives to Achieve Superior Performance.* New York: McGraw-Hill, 2003.

Robert Reich

*Supercapitalism: The Transformation of Business, Democracy, and Everyday Life.* New York: Alfred A. Knopf, 2007.

# Index

"Congress shall make
no law . . . abridging
the freedom of speech,
or of the press."

*First Amendment to the U.S. Constitution*

The basic foundation of our democracy is the First Amendment guarantee of freedom of expression. The Opposing Viewpoints Series is dedicated to the concept of this basic freedom and the idea that it is more important to practice it than to enshrine it.

# Other Books of Related Interest:

**Opposing Viewpoints Series**
Government Spending

**At Issue Series**
What Is the Future of the U.S. Economy?

**Current Controversies Series**
Globalization

# OPPOSING VIEWPOINTS® SERIES

# Corporate Social Responsibility